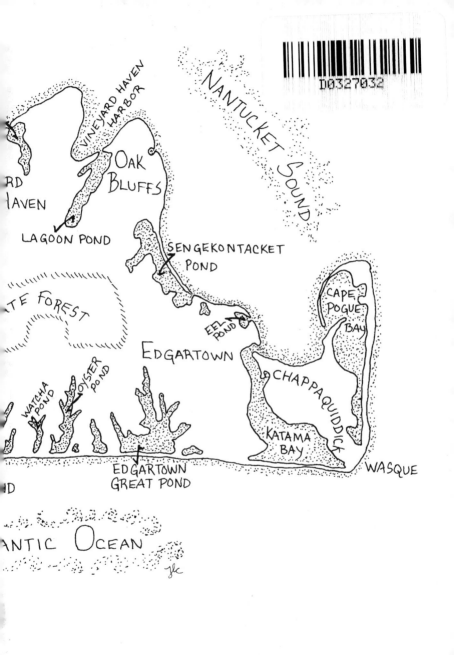

BIRD NEWS

E. VERNON LAUX

Bird News

VAGRANTS AND VISITORS ON
A PECULIAR ISLAND

FOUR WALLS EIGHT WINDOWS

NEW YORK / LONDON

Published in the United States by
Four Walls Eight Windows
39 West 14th Street, room 503
New York, NY 10011
http://www.fourwallseightwindows.com

U.K. offices:
Four Walls Eight Windows/Turnaround
Unit 3 Olympia Trading Estate
Coburg Road, Wood Green
London N22 6TZ

FIRST PRINTING JUNE 1999.

LIBRARY OF CONGRESS CATALOGUING-IN-PUBLICATION DATA
Laux, E. Vernon, 1955-
    Bird news : vagrants and visitors on a peculiar island / by E. Vernon Laux.
        p.   cm.
    ISBN 1-56858-113-0
    1. Bird watching–Massachusetts–Martha's Vineyard.
    2. Birds–Massachusetts–Martha's Vineyard. I. Title.
    QL684.M4L38   1999
    598'.09744'094–DC21   99-33176
                                                       CIP

10 9 8 7 6 5 4 3 2 1

PRINTED IN THE UNITED STATES

Interior design by Elizabeth Elsas
Photos courtesy of E. Vernon Laux
Map of Martha's Vineyard by Janice L. Callaghan

*To the late Richard A. "Bitty" Forster, mentor, friend,
teacher, extraordinary naturalist, and incredible "monster"
of a field man.*

*To the late, great "Big" Ed Laux, a wonderful vibrant
man and great father who let a son follow the path he chose.*

Both men passed much too quickly.

*To my children, Lily and Edward Laux, who have,
no doubt, gone without for their father's fascination and
obsession with winged creatures.*

TABLE OF CONTENTS

Introduction *1*
Migration Overview *5*

Spring *13*
March *19*
April *33*
May *46*

Summer *59*
June *64*
July *77*
August *92*

Hurricane: The Great Undeveloper *106*

Fall *111*
September *115*
October *125*
November *138*

Winter *149*
December *155*
January *166*
February *181*

Martha's Vineyard Chickmouse *195*
Acknowledgments *202*
Martha's Vineyard Birds *208*

The only constant along a beach shoreline is change, much like life itself. Time passes—things change. This is a book about the lives of birds, the miracle and marvel of migration and the passage of time on an island, both seasonally and annually. *Bird News* is also marginally about humans and the great comfort, solace, and pleasure they can derive from the natural world, and from birds in particular. Birds don't always look like the pictures in books—and they rarely stay where they're supposed to. Vagrants, migrants, and hybrids all make the observation of birds and birders unpredictable and exciting.

As the most mobile of all life-forms, birds do something that large terrestrial-dwelling mammals can only imagine: fly. They can and do go where few other creatures can. Birds are found all over the planet, from distant outposts to the largest cities. They are at their most diverse in the equatorial regions of South America, Africa, and Southeast Asia, in terms of numbers of species. But they are even as far-flung as the high Arctic and the shores of Antarctica, where certain breeding colonies exist.

Only two species have been found on the most remote spot on the planet—the South Pole. Inhospitable in every season, Antarctica is the coldest place on Earth. At the South Pole itself, a visitor stands on solid ice almost two miles thick, which stretches to the horizon in every direction. The sky is usually clear, but the surface temperatures range from twenty-three degrees below zero to seventy-six degrees below zero (Fahrenheit) or lower. The nearest unfrozen saltwater may be 900 miles away at the end of the Austral summer in February.

The two types of adventurers here are man and the South Polar skua, a large gull-like bird that is the Antarctic equivalent of a bird of prey. Scientists at the South Pole station thought they were hallucinating when one of these remarkable birds flew overhead and checked them out. Just what the bird was doing miles from any possible food or water is anybody's guess, but perhaps like the land-bound explorers, the bird's curiosity drew it there.

The study of birds can easily become a way of life, as I know all too well. I write about bird life in and around Martha's Vineyard, a roughly 150-square-mile island south of Cape Cod, Massachusetts. In *Bird News*, I've written essays and taken excerpts from some of my columns for the *Martha's Vineyard Gazette*, focusing on happenings ornithologically speaking on the island. Many bird events are universal: migration, breeding, reactions to weather or predators, and nesting. Reading about the particulars of birds on Martha's Vineyard provides a good sense of bird life in general. While birds are nearest and dearest to my heart, I also discuss other winged inhabitants of the Vineyard: bats, dragonflies, and butterflies. After all, the natural world is beautifully interconnected.

Birding is becoming increasingly accessible. There is a wealth of new identification field guides. Binoculars and spotting scopes are more powerful and provide clearer images, allowing us to get an even more accurate bird's-eye view.

I recommend seven to ten power, waterproof, rubberized, close-focusing binoculars. Those that can focus down to four to six feet are critical for adding insects and smaller things to your love of nature. Birding is no longer the exclusive domain of little old ladies in sensible shoes and dottering Englishmen—bird watching has blossomed amongst all ages and fashions! So, plunge into *Bird News*. Pick a section on a favorite season, or the current one. Or just start at the beginning and meander through the passage of a year in the life of these feathered wonders. Remember, keep your eyes to the skies!

Bird migration is one of the most visible and exciting natural phenomena. The distant honking of a flock of geese passing high overhead stirs the blood. The nocturnal flight notes of migrating thrushes, calling to each other as they travel to distant and unknown places, fascinates the earthbound with their ears to the sky. Even more amazing is the sight of a flock of shorebirds, twisting and turning as one, speeding to a destination far from Vineyard shores on an annual pilgrimage that exceeds any other creature's journey.

While superlatives are appropriate, they fail to describe the magic and the awe inspired by spring and fall migration. Twice each year, literally billions of birds—entire species—swarm across the globe, traversing countless thousands of miles as they follow the sun to populate regions only briefly habitable. They bring new meaning to the term *sun worshipping*.

The Vineyard is ideal for migration observation (particularly in the fall), since the island functions as a geographic funnel. It is located south and east of the land mass that makes up the northern half of North America. Many of the birds that nest in Ontario, Quebec, Newfoundland, Nova Scotia, New Brunswick, Maine, New Hampshire, Vermont, New York, and points farther north and west (even Alaska) pass this way in the fall. The Vineyard is also good, in the fall, for western and midwestern bird species because the predominant wind direction (from the northwest) carries the birds south and east. The coast and offshore islands are the last chances for the travelers before a huge obstacle—the ocean. Southbound creatures are rampant, and not just birds. Butterflies, dragonflies, bats, and all manner of winged species are on the move.

As the creatures fight the northwest wind over the ocean, they do a U-turn and attempt to return to the mainland. They move west along the north shore, south shore, and middle of the island. As they reach the island, they proceed to the extreme western tip of the Vineyard and converge on the cliffs at Gay Head. There can be staggering numbers of migrant birds, which makes morning birding at the cliffs the finest in New England. Particularly in late September or October after a cool, northwesterly wind, there is a dazzling display of both rarely seen species and common birds.

Many of the migrants vary their routes in the spring and the fall, in anticipation of the availability of food and ease of passage. A bird's genes contain a wealth of information, including an internal timetable and some navigational expertise. It is truly phenomenal how a warbler or shorebird can return to the same breeding ground each year and then fly many thousands of miles south to winter in exactly the same location as the previous season.

Thanks to the additional young birds, bird populations are at an all-year high in the fall. It is these neophytes, a few months old, that make up the majority of the errant migrants.

Spring migration is not predictable along this coast, and since the birds have been victims of predators all winter, the numbers are smaller. Birds try to stay away from the coastline and stick a few miles inland where food, shelter, and safety are more certain. Since winter has annihilated much of the vegetation needed for consumption or safe camouflage, particularly along the shores, a bird is wise to seek the earlier spring of inland areas. The coastline is nothing but hazardous for the migrant land bird. More birds pass over and through the middle of the country at this season than they do over coastal areas.

In the spring, bird movement is regulated by hormones and species survival imperatives pushing them farther north. Even if bad weather interferes, they urgently continue in order to breed. They want to arrive in plenty of time to take advantage of the best areas and to have as much of the brief summer at their disposal as possible. By early July many shorebirds have already finished their nesting chores for the year and begin moving south. The birds' calendar is different from ours and their survival is dependent on reaching food-rich areas when they are abundantly stocked, not when they are frozen or barren.

With the rapidly shortening fall days and dropping temperatures, conditions to the north of the island become inhospitable for insectivorous birds. Migration gets underway in earnest and the island sees new arrivals daily. Some of the shorebirds may linger for up to three weeks, building their fat reserves. The birds' timetable is more relaxed than in the spring—with the birds lingering, fattening, resting, and waiting for favorable winds. Sandpipers and plovers, for instance, are able to double their body weights quickly. They store the fat so that they are able to metabolize it in flight on the long nonstop journey to the tropics.

Contrary to popular belief, migrant birds are not leading the lives of Riley: half a year's worth of work and then a quick and easy jaunt to six months of fun in the sun. Long-distance migrants endure a rigorous schedule that demands a semiannual journey from the tropics to the northern temperate zones.

Ironically, birders often consider warblers, vireos, flycatchers, and other insectivorous species as "native" birds driven away from their homes by the bitter weather of the northern winter. In fact, most of the species that breed on the Vineyard and all over North America are neotropical migrants who spend far more time in the south win-tering than they do in the north nesting. While many warbler species nest on the Vineyard, arriving with uncanny pre-cision in the first two weeks of May, these birds spend only ten to twelve weeks of the year here. They live twenty-five to thirty weeks in the tropics, with four to six weeks in each direction spent in migration.

Obviously, no layabouts, no idlers allowed.

Of course, not all birds migrate. Most birds living in equatorial regions around the globe are sedentary. They breed during and after wet seasons when insects are most plentiful. About half the 109 species in the New World warbler family breed in North America, north of Mexico. The tyrant flycatchers are one of the most diverse families in the Americas with 370 species currently recognized, but only thirty-five migrate to breed north of Mexico.

The night skies have always been well populated, even before the advent of jet aircraft. Virtually every night in spring and fall, an unseen movement of birds flies over- head. When wind and atmospheric conditions are just right, millions of birds take off at dusk. Most land birds have, in fact, evolved into nocturnal migrants. Diurnal migrants—hawks, storks, pelicans, and gulls—are in the minority. These heavy birds are not designed for flapping flight but instead rely on gliding and soaring. Since air turbulence greatly diminishes when the sun goes down and the sky is relatively calm, soaring birds must utilize daytime air flows.

These large birds keep aloft by seeking and riding ris- ing air currents. There are two kinds: obstruction cur- rents and convection currents, or thermals. Obstruction currents are updrafts caused when a steady or prevailing wind strikes and rises over hills, buildings, ships at sea, or the Gay Head Cliffs. A wind coming down the lee side of a mountain may strike the plain and rebound in a series of "standing waves" each with an updraft component. Thermals are updrafts caused by the uneven heating of air near the surface of Earth. The air over cities or bare fields heats more quickly than the air over forests or bodies of water. Since warm air is lighter, it rises above cool air. Birds are expert at utilizing rising air currents. For instance, the Rift Valley, running from Africa due north into the Middle East to the crossroads of Europe and Asia, is a highway for migrating soaring birds in the spring because of warm air currents rising off the valley floor. Owls are an exception to this general rule. Although owls have high-lift wings, they are not soaring birds—most owls are active and migrate only at night.

Robins, warblers, sparrows, and a multitude of land birds are designed for flapping flight. By flying after the sun goes down, they take advantage of smooth air that enables them to fly with little resistance. They encounter no avian predators until sunrise and they avoid the scorching rays of the sun. They generally wait until a favorable frontal system passes going their way, so to speak, and ascend to their preferred altitude. By flying high they get better tail winds and colder temperatures to help them regulate the generated heat from hard-working flight muscles.

The farther a bird travels in migration, the longer its wings are relative to its body and weight. It's surprising but the size of a bird has little to do with the speed of its flight. A hummingbird, a starling (twenty times as heavy), and a goose (a thousand times as heavy) all have maximum flight velocities of forty-nine to fifty-six miles per hour. For long migration flights, most birds, regardless of size, fly between twenty-seven and forty-two miles per hour. The average flight speed of a migrating land bird is relatively slow.

Since 1940, the study of bird migration has been boosted by radar observation. We are now able to detect the volume, direction, speed, and altitude of migrating birds over land or sea, by day or night, and as far away as sixty miles. But species cannot be identified by radar, and often the radar echoes of small groups of birds cannot be distinguished from individual ones. Even so, this technology has revealed much about migration trends. It also gives us evidence about the destructive nature of human beings and our behavior on natural habitats—both on the ground and in the air.

This knowledge is a challenge to those of us interested in protecting our wildlife. How to address the precipitous decline in migrant bird populations is a constant issue, and how to raise the level of awareness is yet another. These are large problems, indeed, and they urgently need to be tackled. But on a personal level, the marvel of migration is a pleasure to behold, and the sheer magnitude of the journey, as well as the determination of the creatures who undertake it, is a stunning sight in the skies.

Spring

"The sky is the daily
bread of the eyes."
—*Ralph Waldo Emerson*

FOR THOSE OF US INTERESTED IN BIRDS there is no finer way to celebrate the season than on the Vineyard. Every day brings hope, more daylight, and the possibility of species returning to our area. For many, the sight of an osprey coming back from the Gulf of Mexico or Central America is the ultimate triumph of the season. These large, spectacular fish-eating raptors are magnificent to behold. Keep your eyes open at the end of March—many birds are coming our way.

Ornithologically, bad weather with strong winds from any direction offers tremendous excitement. Typically, that means a nor'easter, with howling winds from that direction accompanied by driving rain, sleet, or snow. Occasionally, the propitious weather could be the result of a prolonged period of southwest or western winds that delivers overshoots—migrants that get caught up in strong moving frontal systems and end up farther north than they intended.

Spring on the Vineyard is characterized by daffodils and forsythia, and college students thronging to the place every weekend in search of housing and jobs, in that order. Add to this the people looking at summer rentals or exploring business possibilities and you'll get a Vineyard that is a mad house at every week's end, even before the summer begins. Spring, aka mud season, is closely followed by tick season. Neither is eagerly anticipated by resident or visitor but we must endure these so-called shoulder seasons.

On any walk or drive, you will hear the unmistakable sound that defines a Vineyard spring: spring peeper, a type of tree frog. Although only the size of a thumbnail, these dramatic looking amphibians—spring peepers—are amazingly loud. Pack up the family one early April night and walk until you can't hear anything but the flutelike calls of the peeper drowning out all conversation. Then try to find and catch one, just try!

It is undeniably spring, and most creatures' thoughts do turn to love. On a given evening, listen to the nocturnal calls and courting sounds of the woodcock, known, in some parts of New England, as the timberdoodle. These bizarre sandpipers make a living by probing for earthworms in the leaf litter on the forest floor. About the size of robins, they are camouflaged and literally have their eyes on the tops of their heads. They are unique among shorebirds, since they inhabit the woods. Woodcocks come through in migration, but many also stay to nest and raise their young.

Woodcocks begin displaying on warm nights early in March. The male claims a territory and does an elaborate and noisy courtship demonstration that involves lots of calling, including a sound like "peent." The male then launches into the air and ascends rapidly, making a twittering noise with the feathers on his wings, before he sud-

denly dives towards the ground with another loud noise
emanating from his wings. All is quiet for about thirty seconds, then he yells yet another loud "peent" and starts
over again.

When you tire of woodcock watching and head for
home, you should check your body for those tiny hitch-
hikers—ticks. There are two species prevalent on the
island: the wood tick and the deer tick. It takes twelve to
twenty-four hours for them to get into bloodsucking mode
and that gives you ample opportunity to track down the
little vampires and stake them.

From the initial sighting of the osprey to the viewing of
a myriad of loons, grebes, and sea ducks moving along the
shorelines, from the calls of oystercatchers to the graceful
piping plovers, spring on the island is action packed.
Spring includes doses of cool, damp sea breezes and fog.
Because land reheats faster than the cold seawater, the air
over the land rises, pulling in the denser air from out over
the ocean. This keeps a steady flow of cooler moist ocean
air over the coastline, which retards the development of
vegetation. This causes extreme differences in plant
growth and creates many microclimates, or green spots,
that are easily spotted by birds flying overhead.

These green spots, with accelerated plant growth, are
due to a warmer ambient temperature and protection
from the winds. Think of them as an oasis of leaves, flowers full of sugary sap, and greenery well stocked with juicy
insects and buds, surrounded by a desert of bare-limbed

scrub oak. This is how the island might look to a migrant land bird in the spring. Such an oasis is the best habitat for concentrations of spring migrants.

The entire downtown area of Vineyard Haven is one such spot. Because of the sheltering buildings and the nature of the landscape, this town has a spring much like the rest of the country's. It is at least a full two weeks ahead of anything within a couple of miles of the south shore. On a trip from Vineyard Haven to Gay Head or Chappaquiddick in May, you pass from flowering and fully foliaged shrubs and trees and lush dark grass to somber gray trunks, with catkins swollen and about to emerge, and light green-yellow grass just beginning to grow. And the subtle white bursts of flowering shadbush intermingled into the otherwise stark scrub oak woodland highlight the contrast.

Then comes May, full of predictable as well as unpredictable events. The majority of land bird species migrate away from the coastline and move up the middle of the continent. Yet the resident birds are arriving and there are plenty of surprises. Some years when conditions conspire against the usual migration procedure, there is a memorable fallout of unexpected vagrants along the coast.

March

"Daffodils / That come before the swallow dares / and take the winds of March with beauty." —*William Shakespeare*

MARCH HERALDS THE RETURN of the sun. Day overtakes night in the Northern Hemisphere and by the end of the month, it is more light than dark. Despite occasional setbacks and periods of horrendous weather, things begin to look up. As they say, spring is busting out all over. Skunk cabbage is sprouted and skunks are scavenging hungrily. On warm days, the first butterflies appear. At night, moths begin fluttering about outside lights and car windshields. Buds are ready to burst on red maples, willows, and shrubs growing in the wetlands.

Bird song becomes a regular feature of clear mornings. Resident species are already cranking up the volume and laying claim to territories. Some species will be laying eggs in late March in a mild season. The first returning migrant tree swallows, eastern phoebes, and pine warblers also generally appear the last week of the month.

Blackbirds and robins are already back with more steadily arriving. First, the red-winged blackbirds arrive in late February, followed closely by common grackles. Next to appear are the brown-headed cowbirds and migrant flocks of robins. Resident red-tailed hawks present their aerial demonstrations, and on a sunny day, the sky is filled with song and flight.

Then there are the waters surrounding the island— swarming with migrant loons, grebes, and more. The shoreline is a guiding beacon for northbound flocks of scoters and eiders. Dawn along any shore finds red-throated and common loons winging their way east or north, or perhaps skeins of seas ducks moving to favored feeding grounds, or back to northerly breeding grounds.

The tidal areas are loaded with displaying, courting, and feeding mergansers, goldeneyes, and buffleheads. These ducks are in small flocks, and most are already paired off with their mates. Having selected their partners for the upcoming season, they travel together back to the area where the female was hatched to build a nest and raise a brood. Even the cold sandbars and mudflats are resurgent with piping plovers and oystercatchers. With cold winds blowing and substantial wind chills, the beach may seem inhospitable, but some birds are back. March is a great time to get out there and see what's beginning to happen all around the island.

———

3 MARCH 1995

February was short and sweet. That was a very memorable sunny and mild month, the kind of winter associated with a more southerly latitude. Now with the days length-

ening and temperatures rising, spring is really in the air. It
is very noticeable in the mornings when one arises and
gets out the front door. After months of listening to the
wind in the trees or the passing of a distant auto, there is a
new and welcome sound.

Birds have begun singing again. On a sunny morning,
even if it is below freezing, the sounds of birds reaffirm the
ticking of the annual clock. Vocalizing in a language or
dialect that is specific to each, they are responding to the
end of winter and the beginnings of a new season. Birds
are finely tuned biological marvels, honed by millennia of
evolving and surviving.

Weather influences bird migration in at least four different ways. It controls the advance of the seasons—or the
phenology of natural events—such as the date of the
appearance of the first flowering willow or of the arrival of
the first red-winged blackbirds. Second, it affects the
migrating bird in flight, helping it, hindering it, or even at
times crushing it to Earth. Third, weather may be the
stimulus that initiates the migration journey in a bird
physiologically prepared for it. Finally, operating over
long periods of time, the environmental effects of climate
often become the ultimate determinant in establishing
hereditary tendencies toward migration.

What does all this mean? The first influence, or phe-
nological influence, of weather is ecological. Water birds
gain nothing migrating north in spring if lakes and
streams are still frozen, nor can warblers and flycatchers

survive if there are no insects awaiting them. There are early springs and late springs, and many species adjust their migration schedules to fit the pace of the advancing season. As spring advances northward each year, accompanying and successive waves of ecological phenomena also march northward: the thawing of ice and snow, the first green blades, the emergence of insects and worms, the flowering of trees.

Some birds migrate northward immediately on the heels of minimal spring conditions that allow their survival. The Canada goose pushes northward roughly in step with the advance of the 37 degree Fahrenheit isotherm. Other species, such as the gray-cheeked thrush, wait in their wintering areas until ecological conditions are suitable in the breeding zone; then they migrate north with a rush.

Many studies have been made of the more direct influences of weather on birds while they are migrating. Attempts to correlate migration movements with barometric pressure, wind direction, precipitation, and temperature have resulted in conflicting conclusions. It seems clear, however, that the springtime waves of migrating birds in the eastern United States usually coincide with the flow of warm, moist, southerly winds from the Gulf of Mexico. There is little doubt that adverse weather impedes migration and can cause concentrations of birds to pile up. Storms, strong head winds, or fog ordinarily keep birds grounded. With the return of favorable weather, these birds move on in waves. That is why good birders keep one eye on the weather map.

Early March and this writer is getting itchy for the spring migration. Bird news has been fairly quiet. Both red-winged blackbirds and common grackles have arrived and continue to do so. Waterfowl can be seen pairing off and displaying anywhere one looks.

The 27th had a beautiful sunset and a fabulous display of short-eared owls and harriers hunting and interacting at Katama at dusk.

6 MARCH 1998

The weather has been anything but typical this winter. The past week has been remarkable with temperatures reaching sixty degrees in sheltered areas and the whole progression of the season has advanced so far out of kilter that anything seems possible. It certainly is sending strange signals to plant life and should a stretch of cold, snowy weather hit, as improbable as it seems, it would kill many plants' new growth.

Everything is a little out of synch this year and bird life is no exception. All behavior and migration patterns are accelerated or skewed a bit and this may bode well for the terrestrial bird observer. The weather patterns have been affecting much more than just Martha's Vineyard and many of "our" birds migrate tremendous distances. El Niño generated weather patterns have, or, more likely global warming has, been affecting the entire planet, causing chaos and disaster.

This writer thinks that this spring migration could have all sorts of lost and displaced birds, more rarities could and should appear this spring than ever before. That is what the birder in me hopes for: visions of strange and delightful unknown species flitting from bush to bush and me scrambling for field guides to exotic places in an attempt to put names on unfamiliar species.

The island's rarest bird, the female hermit warbler, was seen again in the state forest in Edgartown over the weekend. This stray warbler from the dense coniferous forests of the Pacific Northwest has delighted birders from all over New England since 21 December 1997. It is a very rare bird in the eastern half of North America.

Because of the advanced season, many wintering birds have moved out from their winter quarters in dense thickets back onto breeding areas. Eastern bluebird males are singing and calling all over the center of the island, defending nesting territories and advertising for a mate. Eastern towhees have begun to sing and are back in areas that they do not winter in. This is all a good four to five weeks earlier than normal.

Mornings have gotten noisy. The level of bird song has increased dramatically this past week. From song and savannah sparrows, along with horned larks singing along the shorelines and, in the dunes, to black-capped chickadees, white-breasted nuthatches, Carolina wrens, and red-bellied woodpeckers in the wooded areas, the island airwaves are jammed with bird songs.

This is the best time of year to learn bird songs and calls for a variety of reasons. There are no leaves on deciduous trees and bushes, allowing for good viewing conditions of the singer. There are not that many different species of birds here now so the choices of what bird is singing are limited and very easily figured out. The ones that are here are common, mostly year-round residents, whose song once learned will be a constant source of pride.

Learning bird vocalizations is the best way to locate birds throughout the year. It also eliminates the need to go crashing into and through impenetrable thickets, marshy bogs, and dense woodlands, scaring and chasing wildlife away. If you remain still and listen, you can't miss the resident bird species singing and calling, especially first thing in the morning from March into July.

Migrants that have arrived and are pushing into the area include common grackles, red-winged blackbirds, and American robins. The vanguard arrived a couple of weeks ago but now these species are literally everywhere. Robins, while wintering in small numbers, are now on lawns, fields, and even the woods as these hardy birds move north along with warmer temperatures.

Matt Pelikan was out up-island in Gay Head and Chilmark on the 27th and found seventy-five red-throated loons, ten red-necked grebes, sixty horned grebes, a sharp-shinned hawk, thirty harlequin ducks, twenty-five

purple sandpipers, 125 Bonaparte's gulls, twenty razorbills, many bluebirds, and a palm warbler catching flies off
the eaves of a house. Matt predicted that mourning cloak
butterflies would be seen any day and spent a good deal of
time looking for one in February. On the 28th, the last day
of the month and, the second sunny morning in a row,
success was realized when he found not one but two of
these large and stunningly beautiful butterflies. They are
amazing to behold in an otherwise dreary winter landscape. They were flying and sunning themselves on the
edge of a path at Menemsha Hills in Chilmark.

14 MARCH 1997

Spring is such a protracted, nebulous affair on the island
that this writer prefers to think of the island as having
three seasons and a fourth category known as the mud
season. Mud season usually begins in early March and
continues until early May. On some roads it is much
longer. The mud season has started and for those who live
down any long dirt or mud road, which are plentiful at
this time of year, this category needs no explanation.

What this might have to do with birds is a fair question. Birders are by their nature highly migratory and
curious about things all around them. Busybody might be
another word to use. Birders want to know what is going
on outside—in the trees, in the fields, on the pond, and
even on the waters surrounding the island. Birders invari-
ably end up on the nastiest, muddiest tracks on the Vineyard and are forever in need of the services of a tow truck.

When asked what they are doing in this incredible quagmire passing itself off as a road, they reply "looking for birds." Inquiring minds want to know.

There is a dramatic change out of doors happening every morning. Bird song is increasing daily. As the days lengthen, birds' endocrine systems are getting in gear for the nesting season. For resident species like cardinals, chickadees, and song sparrows this means getting up early and defending a territory. They do this by what we call singing but which is a mechanism used by the birds to advertise to others that this lot is taken, look elsewhere.

This method of spatial separation works well. Any area that has suitable habitat that is not occupied will be quickly transformed into a breeding area if the population has surplus individuals. The lack of a singing male defending the area is like a neon sign to other males of that species that the area is ripe for the taking.

The end of the winter is a hard time for many species, especially raptors, birds that make their living by capturing other live animals. Generally only healthy birds and mammals survive the winter to this point and they are adept at avoiding predators. The hawks and owls have to work that much harder to capture food and their lives hang on their ability to get that next meal. They are remarkable for the precision and determination they bring to the task.

There is nothing comparable in excitement to watching a hawk in pursuit of its prey. Twisting and turning at terrific speeds, hawks' prey usually escapes. But on average, out of ten such attacks one will end with the capture of a meal for the hawk.

On the 10th, Arnold Brown heard a loud noise and witnessed a Cooper's hawk attacking and capturing a starling off his bird feeder from a mere four feet away. The young bird with a brown-streaked chest came rocketing in and snagged the starling with one foot armed with powerful talons. Both birds crashed to the ground, out of Arnold's view, and the hawk finished off the starling. By the time Arnold got to the door, the hawk was mantling the starling, but obviously winded. Within thirty seconds, two crows, which were slightly larger than the hawk, were harassing the hawk in an attempt to steal the hard-won prize. The hawk had enough strength left to make off with the bird.

26 MARCH 1999

Two eagerly anticipated events occurred recently. The arrival of spring on the Vineyard and the return of the osprey. These events occur fairly close together every year. In this last spring of the century, the birds beat the arrival of spring by two days arriving on the 18th.

Ospreys are large, black-and-white hawks with various populations found worldwide. The birds that breed on the island and in the northeast United States winter from the Gulf Coast, around islands in the Caribbean, along both coasts of Mexico and Central America, and northern South America.

The species has adapted to weather and food resources

by developing a schedule that is as perfect as nature allows. They arrive just as countless anadromous fish move inshore and make their way back to natal streams. The older, more experienced birds know the best places to find fish.

They feed exclusively on live fish that they capture in spectacular fashion by stooping from high above the water and throwing their talons forward at the last possible millisecond, crashing feet-first into the water. Individual success rates per dive are highly variable.

In most years, a couple of male ospreys arrive ahead of the crowd. Then more trickle in gradually over the following days and females arrive shortly thereafter. By early April all returning adults from the previous nesting season should be back at their respective sites. This year the birds arrived en masse. There were no birds seen or reported on Saint Patrick's Day. On the 18th, there were no fewer than fifteen reports of ospreys from locations scattered across the island. This is a first in this writer's experience.

Many bird species are on the move. Overwintering species are moving out and breeding residents are returning. A lone snow goose has been widely reported from the fields at the Keith Farm in Chilmark. American oyster-catchers have started to trickle in.

Tree swallows are showing up in small numbers and will increase daily. Look for returning swallows of several species over fresh water ponds on sunny mornings. Almost any freshwater pond with emerging insects will attract early season swallows. Tree swallows are normally the first to arrive, followed closely by barn, rough-winged, and bank swallows. Purple martins may also appear.

Strong southwest winds or northeast winds associated with fast moving frontal systems coming from the Gulf Coast are what the weather-watching birder is hoping for at this season. Many southern herons and virtually all migrant land birds may appear during or following these conditions.

Lastly, a flock of about thirty-five Bonaparte's gulls was graced by the presence of an adult little gull on the afternoon of the 23rd off East Chop in Oak Bluffs. This appropriately named smallest of all gull species is a great- looking bird with jet black underwings set against a white-and-gray overall color. It is dainty on the wing with relatively rounded wings. It is about the size of a common tern and even smaller than the tiny Bonaparte's gulls. Little gulls are always scarce in and around the island and this one was headed west in Vineyard Sound and obviously migrating north with the Bonaparte's gulls.

29 MARCH 1996

Birds are seemingly everywhere at the end of March. All songbirds that spent the winter here are cranking up and getting the rust off the syrinx. Woodpeckers seem particularly rambunctious, as is their nature, and they are hammering away on everything from antennae to house trim, much to the chagrin of the human occupants.

The biggest culprit for loud banging is the largest woodpecker found on the Vineyard, the northern flicker. These handsome woodpeckers with striking markings and bright white rump patches are common and widespread on the island. Several complaints have been called into the bird line about flickers hammering on metal sheathing and telephone poles. The object for the woodpeckers is to make the loudest noise possible and they are experts at amplification.

While flickers are making a lot of noise they are not alone, as all the other woodpeckers that live on the Vineyard are also engaged in the spring "drum-off." Red-bellied, hairy, and downy woodpeckers are all making a racket and a walk almost anywhere in wooded areas is sure to demonstrate all four species of woodpeckers drumming and calling. Since there are no leaves on the deciduous trees, it is easy to get a look at them and also to watch the interactions between individuals as they engage in display and defense of territories in preparation for breeding.

Black-capped chickadees are busy calling while searching for nest holes. The island population of these birds is unique. From Maine to the state of Washington, from Nova Scotia to British Columbia, this widespread species has a distinct two-note song—deee-deee—with the first note distinctly higher than the second. The birds on the Vineyard have developed their own distinct tune, with both whistled notes on exactly the same pitch, at least to the human ear. This interesting phenomena has come to the attention of scientists. Early in the month of May, a group of researchers armed with directional microphones, advanced tape recording equipment, and lots of stamina will arrive to study and record our chickadees. This will be the third year of this project and they are also attempting to get recordings from birds in nearby Woods Hole and neighboring islands Nantucket, the Elizabeth Islands, and Block Island. With more information about these geographically isolated and probably reproductively isolated populations of chickadees, they hope to make sense out of what is happening.

New birds continue to arrive and many species appear to be on a record-setting pace for arriving a bit ahead of schedule. Piping plovers, American oystercatchers, and ospreys all arrived earlier than had ever been recorded. This past week another familiar spring migrant that usually arrives late in April appeared staggeringly early at the feeder of Janet and Rick Bayley. Watching their feeder the morning of the 20th, they noticed a strikingly colored small finch. It was a brilliant, deep blue and they quickly recognized it as an indigo bunting.

Indigo buntings are fairly common in Massachusetts as nesting birds and are frequently encountered in migration. They do not breed on the Vineyard, but often are here in big numbers in the spring and again in the fall.

APRIL

"The sun was warm but the wind was chill./You know how it is with an April day/When the sun is out and the wind is still/You're one month on in the middle of May/But if you so much as dare to speak/A cloud comes over the sunlit arch/A wind comes off a frozen peak/And you're two months back in the middle of March." —*Robert Frost*

APRIL IS A MONTH OF EXTREMES — anything is possible from dramatic swings in temperature to shifting wind velocities and sky conditions, including a capricious mix of precipitation. As the New England adage goes, if you don't like the weather—wait a minute. The moderating influence of the surrounding cold water makes April very slow to warm up and often downright cold. A walk on the beach may require a parka, hat, and gloves, or alternatively, a T-shirt and shorts.

The dawn chorus has begun in earnest and the tunes don't die out until the day itself does. Robins, cardinals, song sparrows, eastern towhees, pine warblers, nuthatches, four species of woodpeckers, and virtually all resident species that have wintered or arrived are singing and defending territories. Woodcock are performing their nightly courtship flights in fields islandwide. And the spring peeper cacophony acts as a beacon for the frogs to locate vernal ponds. It is the call for an annual rite of spring, a frog orgy, if you will.

A ride on the ferry is a natural history extravaganza with flocks of scoters, eiders, mergansers, migrating loons, and grebes overhead. Often on morning trips, you can see as many as several thousand scoters of all three species.

The beach may be cold at this season but it's far from dreary. Common and red-throated loons, horned and a few red-necked grebes, common eiders, black, surf, and white-winged scoters, red-breasted mergansers, all sorts of other ducks, and the occasional oddity are visible to anyone glancing above them. Northern gannets—spectacular, large white birds with black wing tips—fly and plunge, diving headlong into the water with a huge splash.

On days when the wind is not howling or at dawn and dusk when the water is like a mirror, common loons give their unmistakable call of the wild. Their movements are graceful and surprisingly rapid, their plumage is intricately patterned, and their yodeling communicates deeply felt, universal messages.

Another feature of April, often after periods of sustained southwesterly winds, is the premature appearance of many southern species, including prothonotary warblers, summer tanagers, blue grosbeaks, indigo buntings, and several other Central American winterers. Many never intended to come this far north. While this is exciting for the observer, it can be dire for the birds—many perish.

11 APRIL 1997

April arrived like a wounded bear bringing a savage
nor'easter that dumped snow and wrought devastation all
through southern New England. Sadly, one of the best
naturalists in the country, a man with an encyclopedic
knowledge of all flying things in New England and Massachusetts, a great field man, was also stopped by the freak-
ish storm. He was a one-man resource who freely gave of
his knowledge, experience, and quick wit. Richard A.
Forster of Wellesley, Massachusetts was stricken while
shoveling snow on the afternoon of the 1st and expired.
He was well known and loved by a wide array of people
and was, at the time of his death, the main man in matters
pertaining to birds, butterflies, dragonflies, and wild flowers. He will be sorely missed by his many island friends
and all who knew him.

April Fool's Day was mostly but not all bad news and
birds of note have begun to appear. On the 1st, at a feeder
in West Tisbury, was a striking male yellow-throated warbler. John Bryant, a wood carver extraordinaire of birds,
particularly warblers, noticed this bird coming to his sunflower and put binoculars on it. His surprise was complete when he saw that it was a warbler he had never
encountered on the Vineyard.

Another (or the same) yellow-throated warbler, a male
with unmistakable plumage characters, was found on the
7th at West Chop Woods by Arnold Brown. The presence
of two of these southern warblers is extremely unusual.
Incongruously, warbler species with a southern range

migrate north ahead of more northerly nesting species. Their appearance in New England is often in late March, April, and early May before the arrival of migrant species that are proceeding farther north to breeding areas that are last to become hospitable for the insectivorous birds.

A blue-gray gnatcatcher—a marvelous little bird with subtle colors, an eye-ring, a long tail with white outer rectrices, and an almost insectlike buzz call—was heard and then seen at the end of West Chop in Vineyard Haven on the 8th. This makes it the earliest spring record for the state and a significant record for the island.

Land birds are beginning to appear in migrant traps. In spring, a migrant trap here is anywhere that leafs out first. Emergent vegetation with its attendant flowers, nectar, and most importantly insects is the "bait" that attracts passing migrants.

On the 1st, a rare spring flock of lapland longspurs was found in the white-out conditions at Katama by this writer and Lanny McDowell. There were twenty birds and the males were in breeding plumage. This is a plumage rarely seen in these parts and this was the first flock of these birds ever seen in spring on the island.

Andy Goldman and wife Susan watched a turkey vulture fly about their bluff in Chilmark for most of the day on the 4th. The bird landed on a nearby roof and intently watched the place, affording great views of its head and nostrils to the couple. Andy surmises that the bird could smell the suet in the feeders and was trying to figure out how to get at it. Vultures have highly developed olfactory senses and experiments have proven that they can and do locate food by smell alone — finding buried carcasses under the rain forest canopy in the neotropics. Nothing like the smell of suet.

This last week an unprecedented incursion of monarch butterflies was noted. On the 7th, Paul Jackson was floored by the sight of one of these nectaring at vinca flowers in West Tisbury along with a painted lady and a mourning cloak. Arnold and Edie Brown watched one in Vineyard Haven and this writer saw one flying out over the outer harbor from the ferry *Islander*. It appears as though a flight of these insects was migrating north well ahead of schedule.

Tony and Sally Marucca of Vineyard Haven have seen a chukar in their yard. This grayish brown game bird has been widely introduced into North America and is frequently seen on Chappy. This is a first report for Vineyard Haven and who knows where it came from.

12 *April 1996*
Winter weather refuses to leave as the island was hit by two unseasonable storms, enduring yet more snow, this time in April. Temperatures dropped and winter storm advisories were posted on three days last week. High winds and cold temperatures destroyed those ambitious gardeners' hopes of an early crop and many seedlings optimistically planted were destroyed. This weather is also extremely hazardous to migrant birds.

Many early arriving species are susceptible to cold,

wind, storms, and consequent lack of insect food. Eastern phoebes, tree swallows, egrets, indigo buntings, and any early moving land birds run a big risk by arriving before temperatures have moderated for good. Even some of the hardier species, like ospreys and piping plovers, can experience great difficulty in obtaining food. Albert Fischer found a dead great egret on the beach in Gay Head on 23 March.

Most amazing was a lone male parula warbler seen by Ed and Maggie Sibert and Linda Carruthers on 28 March at Sheriff's Meadow Pond in Edgartown. This neotropical wintering migrant normally arrives at the beginning of May. This sighting represents the earliest arrival date for this species seen alive in Massachusetts. It was not seen again. This bird is very unlikely to have survived the inclement weather. The previous earliest spring record was of a bird found dead on 1 April 1978 over in Westport, Massachusetts.

Raptors—hawks and owls—are a treat and virtually impossible to miss on the island in April. Ospreys and red-tailed hawks can be seen engaged in spectacular aerial maneuvers as they court potential mates and run off competitors. Loops, rolls, grappling and falling, dives and amazing stoops can all be seen. Just stake out an osprey's pole (with a nest) with a good view and watch the goings-on.

Short-eared owls have been regular at dusk in the fields at Katama. Joe Cressy watched five individual owls hunting and interacting with several harriers on the evening of the 8th. At 3:30 on the afternoon of the 9th, two short-ears were out hunting actively in the relative calm and overcast before the storm. By 5:30 it was snowing heavily. The short-ears got into several battles with resident harriers. The hawks do not want the owls hunting over their breeding territories and are beginning to get serious about defending them. These short-eared owls are going to migrate north a couple of thousand miles to breeding grounds on the summer tundra.

Turkey vultures have also been very much in evidence the past couple of weeks. Reports of singles and of a couple have been widespread from Gay Head to Chappaquiddick. These primarily warm weather birds have been moving slowly northward for the past decade and are now commonly breeding throughout New England. The first nest on the Vineyard was discovered four years ago over on the north side not far from Cedar Tree Neck in West Tisbury. It seems as though the vultures are still increasing and they are reported almost year-round.

The shorelines have been very active. Red-throated and common loons are moving by in some numbers. Northern gannets have been common along the south shore and Wasque has been spectacular with hundreds of these large plunge divers fishing the rips. Eiders and scoters are moving in large flocks, and if the weather is nice, a trip to look for ducks can be very rewarding.

14 APRIL 1995

Spring, the most unpredictable of seasons on the island, proved it again. The past week brought temperatures ranging up and down the thermometer, winds from all points on the compass, and some very exciting bird sightings. The number of calls to the twenty-four-hour bird hot line was impressive as was the quality of the birds. In keeping with the general trend to date this year, there were some exceptionally early migrants reported.

Topping the list of early returns was an eastern kingbird seen in Gay Head on the 10th. These tyrant flycatchers are among the more conspicuous and pugnacious of our nesting land birds, building bulky nests in trees. They normally arrive the first week of May.

Albert Fischer also spotted a group of six barn swallows on the 6th in Gay Head. They normally arrive mid- to late April and are another case of the early bird, hopefully, finding the worm, so to speak. The trade-off is that nasty weather could limit food and mean death.

A little blue heron was found by Matthew Dix on the 10th at Priester's Pond in West Tisbury. This beautiful southern heron is always uncommon-to-rare on the Vineyard, spring sightings more on the rare side. Matthew was looking at a couple of pairs of green-winged teal when he noticed the little blue along the shoreline. As this is MV land bank property, it is accessible to any who have the inclination to go look.

The first snowy egret of the spring was seen on the 11th in Gay Head by Albert Fischer. Egrets normally arrive in early April or even late March, so it is perfectly on time. He also reports that up to four American oystercatchers have been calling and flying about over Squibnocket Pond in both Chilmark and Gay Head and notes that they have never done this before in the spring. Perhaps the first up-island pair is about to establish themselves.

Jan Callaghan was birding in Chilmark on the 8th and spotted her first harlequin ducks, not one but thirty-two of them. These incredible ducks rank among the most beautiful waterfowl in the world. She also spotted a male kestrel nearby. Bob and Fran Clay were active over the last weekend on Chappaquiddick. On the 9th they noted a pair of harriers, three killdeer, eastern bluebirds, tree swallows, white-throated sparrows, and a singing pine warbler. One of the earliest songbird migrants in Massachusetts was spotted by Tom Rivers on the 10th in Chilmark. The ruby-crowned kinglet usually appears in the first two weeks of April, so it is nice to see a migrant doing what is expected of it. Eastern phoebes have returned according to several reports.

24 *APRIL* 1998

This is an exciting time of year. The greening of the plants is well along and colors not seen for many months appear more vivid than remembered. As April proceeds and gives way to May, a mixed bag of more and varied species arrive to nest on the island, accompanied by many more individuals that are passing through on their way to breeding grounds farther north.

Long-distance neotropical migrants, as well as species

that only move a few hundred miles or overwinter, are all
undergoing changes. They are molting body feathers and
changing plumage, getting ready for the breeding season.
For example, take the eastern towhee that winters in thickets in small numbers on the island. This wintering population, if they survive the rigors of winter, has the early
jump on the best breeding territories. The bulk of the
population arrives in numbers beginning in early to mid-
April, becoming one of the most abundant and common
breeding birds on Martha's Vineyard.

Until recently this bird was known as the rufous-sided
towhee. But after further research into the western form, it
was proven that the two races of what was formerly called
rufous-sided towhee are distinct populations and quite
different in plumages and range, so scientists split them
into two separate species. Vineyard and eastern birds
were labeled eastern towhee and the western birds are
called spotted towhees. The eastern towhees have arrived
and their distinctive "chewink" calls and "drink your tea"
songs are emanating from trees and bushes islandwide.

The most unusual bird spotted this week was a yellow-
billed cuckoo seen by Lou Hathaway on the 18th in
Ocean Heights in Edgartown. Occasionally, in spring after
coastal storms or movements they appear in April. The
last one to do so on the Vineyard was 27 April 1980 on
Chappaquiddick.

This individual appeared sick or tired and no doubt
was lucky to find a landfall. Lou had never seen one

before, but the bird cooperated in the extreme by being tame and obligingly foraging for food right in one of Lou's window boxes. The same weather that delivered this bird to the island also brought many others.

Highlights included calling common loons off the Chop, numerous tree swallows, a group of barn swallows, three rough-winged swallows, a rare April cliff swallow, four ruby-crowned kinglets, approximately 100 yellow-rumped warblers, fifteen pine warblers, four palm warblers, the first four black-and-white warblers, a singing common yellowthroat, many white-throated sparrows in an array of plumages, and a single male blue grosbeak that was observed fly-catching on a rooftop. The bird was all brown with the distinctive prominent rusty wing bars, sideways tail twitch, and just the beginning of blue on the head and face. Another couple of weeks and this individual will be shockingly deep blue with two rusty wing bars. This is a rare bird in Massachusetts and always a nice find on the island in the spring.

26 *APRIL 1996*

Already the last weekend in April and the birding is starting to heat up. One of the best kept secrets in Massachusetts ornithology is the spectacular number of migrant loons that pass along the south shore of the Vineyard in mid- to late April. Hundreds and even thousands of red-throated loons wing their way east along the south shore from dawn until midmorning.

The birds are literally everywhere, swimming on the water's surface and flying close to shore and as far as one can see to the horizon. Mixed in with all these red-throated loons are common loons, some horned grebes, a mixture of various sea ducks, northern gannets, gulls, and occasionally alcids or some surprise bird.

A warbler that is always rare on the Vineyard was discovered. And when it rains it pours because not only was one bird found but possibly two individuals. This all happened on 20 April. Surprisingly, this rare bird was found by two separate observers at different times in locations that were only a few miles apart in Oak Bluffs.

Worm-eating warblers breed in dense understory on dry wooded hillsides. They are a rather rare nester in Massachusetts with a pair here and there in the eastern part of the state with the highest density occurring around Mount Tom in central Massachusetts. They are a rare migrant on the Vineyard and much more likely to be encountered in the fall migration than the spring.

Dave Small from Athol, Massachusetts, who regularly participates on the Vineyard Christmas Count, was visiting and went for an early morning walk along the back of Farm Pond in Oak Bluffs. Here he was amazed to find a worm-eating warbler feeding along the ground. Realizing its rarity, he headed back to get some other observers but when he returned, the bird had vanished.

Around noon on this same day, Allan Keith from Chilmark stopped by the Oak Bluffs pumping station to see if the pine siskins were still there. After locating some siskins, he was amazed and excited about finding a worm-eating warbler feeding on the ground in the dense under-story about a hundred yards along the entrance road. My opinion is that it was the same bird, which moved over to the superior habitat available at the head of the lagoon. Many birds move along the shores of the lagoon, and the pumping station has proven time and again that it is the premiere Vineyard locale for spring migrants, especially insectivorous vireos and warblers.

Indigo buntings appeared from Gay Head to Chap-paquiddick this past week. Matthew Dix was walking his dog on the 19th when he saw a woodcock put on an awe-some double-broken-wing act. The bird flopped on the ground and thrashed about as if it were seriously injured, to lure Matthew and his dog away from something. This bird must have been incubating a clutch of eggs, and dog or human must have been close to the well-disguised nest. Neat way to see one of these improbable and bizarre birds.

MAY

"It's May, it's May, the lusty month of May!" — *Lerner & Lowe*

THE RETURN OF THE MIGRANT BIRDS to their familiar breeding ground, whether it be sand bar, field, or woodland, is a celebration of the instincts of reproduction. Despite the vagaries of weather, they alight on the island with remarkable precision and punctuality. Their timing, one could say without hyperbole, is impeccable.

Every day in May is an adventure. Terns take up residence on beaches and promptly begin courtship flights and displays. It is a shifting of gears in the cycle of life. Birds of many species are plentiful, colorful, and noisy.

The din of bird song that greets the dawn increases during the month and reaches its zenith in early to mid-June. The males are the primary songsters—busy marking their territory—since the females have more important things to do: nesting, laying eggs, and incubating them. When the eggs hatch, the insatiable nestlings require considerable nourishment, and then the turf becomes critical. Individuals with too small an area will not be able to feed the young, and those with good foraging habitat will.

May is a good month to rise early and get out-of-doors.

On a gray, wet morning with easterly winds, there is little point in looking for warblers, because their insect food is not hatching and they will be lying low. But a look off the southeast corner of Wasque at first light will be rewarding. You encounter seabirds that drifted towards shore, pushed westward during the night by the wind and accompanying driving rain. At dawn they get off the surface, look around, don't like what they see, and then return to the open ocean and preferred feeding areas. It is easier to detect many species in the spring, since they are in brilliant breeding plumage and quite vocal. The ruddy turnstones are positively gaudy as they constantly feed, fueling themselves for the final flight to high Arctic nesting areas. Around island shores, there continues to be one of the largest concentrations of sea ducks in the spring anywhere.

May is also the last month before the exploding human population of the Vineyard makes it difficult to bird. The first taste of things to come is over the Memorial Day weekend. The island is jammed with people. But it is also traditionally a great time for birding, with the greatest diversity of species and the possibility of strays.

---

1 *MAY 1998*

The last week of April found three species of grosbeak visiting island feeders. The word grosbeak enters English from the French *grosbec* meaning "thick-billed," as these birds are. Debbie and Jason Carter and family discovered a strange-looking bird at their feeder on the 26th at Katama in Edgartown. Looking in their field guide, they noted the size, big bill, blue color, and two prominent rusty wing bars. They confidently and correctly identified the bird as a blue grosbeak. The bird was a male that was changing from its winter brown to summer blue and in heavy molt. It didn't really look like any of the plates in the book because it was in transition plumage. This species is found south and west of here. It is always a rare bird on the island.

The second kind of grosbeak seen was found by Susan Heilbron in Chilmark on the 25th. Looking out her kitchen window, she was startled by the appearance of a brilliantly marked, yellow and black bird larger than the goldfinches, housefinches, and other birds at the feeders. She looked it up and discovered she was clearly looking at a male evening grosbeak. This species is to the grosbeaks and feeder birds what the oystercatcher is to the beach—a serious crowd pleaser. It is a nomadic northern finch and is extremely irruptive and downright weird in its appearances.

The third species of grosbeak is an annual visitor to spring bird feeders on the Vineyard. Rose-breasteds are as boldly marked as the other species. But every spring is different and they never seem to appear at the same place twice. Susan Yurkus of Oak Bluffs and Mary Jackson of Edgartown both have male rose-breasted grosbeaks at their respective feeders. These gaudy birds are quite different than the females, as is true of most grosbeaks. The dimorphic plumages make it very easy, at least in the spring, to sex individual birds as the males and females are totally different.

Mary Jane Pease of Chilmark reported a hummingbird in her yard on the 28th. This is the first report of the year. She also is delighted to report having a nesting pair of eastern bluebirds.

Andy Goldman, guests Justin Lavigne and Lily Laux from Great Barrington, Massachusetts, and this writer were treated to a ride in Andy's able boat the *Heritage* on the morning of the 26th. The route was out of Menemsha to Quick's Hole, the wide passage between Nashaweena and Pasque Island, along the north shore of Nashaweena, into Cuttyhunk and then back to Menemsha. The weather was not very nice and drizzle, then rain started about halfway through the trip and the wind came up.

A remarkable gathering of sea ducks was found feeding and resting along the west side of and at the northern end of the channel. This is obviously an important staging area for migrant sea ducks and little is known about it. The birds move north from here overland across Rhode Island and southeastern Massachusetts or across Cape Cod on their flight to tundra breeding areas.

5 *MAY* 1995

Things are starting to heat up—both literally and figuratively. If one is afflicted with birding aspirations, the month of May is one of the two peak months.

The ever-increasing day length, increasing air and water temperatures, and greening of the land mark the beginning of the breeding season both here and increasingly farther north. Most piping plovers are already incubating eggs on the beaches. This endangered species has responded well to increased protection and is doing very well on island beaches.

American oystercatchers are also incubating and these large colorful shorebirds can be seen vigorously defending their nesting areas from both great black-backed and herring gulls, and pesky crows. These species would love to make a meal of the oystercatchers' eggs and or young but oystercatchers are fierce. This writer has seen an oystercatcher out fly a gull, land on its back traveling at about fifty miles an hour, and begin tearing feathers out of its back and neck with its beak. The gull certainly did not enjoy this as the oystercatcher's beak is a brilliantly colored shucking knife, so it departed hastily.

Aside from all the returning summer resident species were a few unexpected and brilliantly colored individuals. Most conspicuous was a male prothonotary warbler seen on the 28th in Major's Cove, on Sengekontacket Pond right on the Edgartown/Oak Bluffs town line. John Pierson noticed this bird land on his feeder and realized immediately that it was something very different. While he was reaching for a field guide, the bird flew off the feeder and collided with a sliding glass door, stunning itself. This afforded excellent views of this striking golden yellow warbler with blue-gray wings. After a couple of minutes, the bird snapped out of it and flew off, not to be seen again.

Also on the 30th was an unusual sighting of a flock of migrant willets. These birds are probably en route to Nova Scotia where a population of these salt marsh-loving shorebirds breed. Occasionally in mid- to late April, especially when grounded by rain and fog, migrant flocks will appear on the islands. It is always a rare treat to actually see them.

17 MAY 1996

The next ten days are as good as it gets for birding in the spring on the Vineyard. As the spring migration comes to a close at the end of May, birds push northward in a frantic final dash to their breeding grounds. Almost all small birds migrate at night at high altitude.

As they fly in loose groups calling to each other in the dark, they are susceptible to any vagaries of wind drift and obscuring phenomena (clouds and fog). When it begins to get light, they look for suitable habitat and descend to feed and rest for the day.

This is the time when the greatest number of species can be seen on the Vineyard. It is possible to hear many species of birds before it gets light in the morning—a trick that is impossible to duplicate in the fall migration. It is the time for a birdathon—a twenty-four-hour attempt to go all out and find as many different species as possible in any chosen area.

The record for the Vineyard is 144 species in a single

day and that was recorded in late May about six years ago. This Saturday, the 18th, an attempt to surpass this record will be afoot. All eyes are on the weather map hoping for strong southwesterly winds with some kind of frontal system arriving just before it to ground all northbound migrants and hopefully some overzealous southerly breeders. The best conditions would be warm temperatures with little or no wind for owling, whip-poor-wills and chuck-wills-widow, bird song, and land birding.

The bird line went wild this past week with over thirty calls from a diverse group of people. Baltimore orioles and rose-breasted grosbeaks are at feeders from Gay Head to Chappaquiddick. The orioles both migrate through and nest on the Vineyard so some are probably migrants and others are setting up territories. The rose-breasted grosbeaks are not known to breed on the island but are widespread nesters in deciduous forests not far away on the mainland. White-crowned sparrows have made a welcome spring appearance.

Ingrid "Ting" Thomas had great views of a male scarlet tanager that was around her place in Edgartown from the 8th until the 12th. Great egrets have been seen in a couple of places. These large white herons with black legs and feet and yellow bills are impressive to see. Gus Daniels and Jerry McCarthy found a northern waterthrush and the first reported veery of the season on the 14th at the Oak Bluffs pumping station at the head of the lagoon. The veery, a thrush that is never common on the Vineyard, was a new or "life" bird for Jerry.

Surprise Spring Fallout
Island Crowded With Birds in Record-Breaking Spring Flight

"Absolutely stunning," "spectacular," and "once in a lifetime" were just a few descriptions thrown out by island birders after a seemingly miraculous flight of birds on the evening of the 18th and early morning of the 19th. Martha's Vineyard was inundated with birds in the finest spring flight of migrants ever recorded in the long and rich island ornithological history. The island, from the Gay Head Cliffs to Cape Pogue on Chappaquiddick, was literally swarming with birds. Unheard of numbers of thrushes, warblers, vireos, orioles, tanagers, and grosbeaks were seen by jubilant observers.

The morning of the 19th dawned rather drearily except for the fact that birds of every description were swarming in the trees and bushes. The grounding of northbound birds was extremely impressive. What made this all the more shocking was the fact that these beautifully colored, brilliant birds were in trees with little or no vegetation. The leaves were not out yet so that the birds were not only easy to see, but they resembled fast-moving Christmas tree ornaments. People were spiritually awakened by strikingly colored birds they had never seen before. One birder called his wife on a cellular phone and said to forget church this morning as there were birds dripping from the trees. Another birder nearby overheard and yelled, "Tell her God is on East Chop this morning!"

In North America large spring flights of northbound

migrants occur with some regularity along the Gulf Coast
States and in green spots in the middle of large urban areas
like Central Park in New York City or Mount Auburn Cemetery in Cambridge. As daybreak approaches, the night-flying
northbound birds look down for suitable resting and feeding
habitat and, if over, say New York City, they have little choice
but to head for the one large green patch, Central Park.
Then every tree in the park is chock-full of birds. That is
exactly what happened on the Vineyard on Sunday, 19 May
1996, a now famous date in the annals of Vineyard bird history. For the first time the twenty-four-hour bird line tape ran
out of room from the volume of calls. Dawn at East Chop
near the lighthouse was unbelievable. Birds were swarming
about in every tree with mixed flocks comprised of some
twenty-two species of warblers, six species of vireos, veeries,
and Swainson's thrushes, scarlet tanagers, rose-breasted
grosbeaks, and many others. At one point, in one field of
view in the binoculars were seven species of warblers.

The warblers are the jewels of the bird world. In spring,
in their breeding plumages, they are colorful, exotic, and
vibrant not only in color, but in movement. With names like
blackburnian, magnolia, Canada, black-throated green,
black-throated blue, bay-breasted, and chestnut-sided, they
are what every birder hopes to see but rarely does. On this
day the birds were impossible to miss. Birds that would
normally be cause for celebration were not even getting a
second look.

On the night of the 18th countless numbers of migrants
came riding the warm front north. The warm air was flowing

from the southwest heading northeast and at the coastline the temperature difference created fog. This caused the birds to misjudge where they were flying. Riding the light winds, many of the birds came farther east than they intended and ended up on the Vineyard by accident.

While a bonanza for birders, it is a bittersweet occurrence. There can be little doubt that a great many migrants perished by falling into the cold Atlantic.

Observers on Cape Pogue watched in amazement as birds came out of the fog into the green oasis near the lighthouse. Along the south shore of the island where spring is always retarded, birds were seen in trees that had not begun to have leaves. Even late in the day exhausted birds were seen landing in leafless trees and shrubs along the shoreline. These birds had gotten so far out to sea that they flew not only all night but all day to get back to land. These were the lucky ones.

For the birds, this day will live in infamy, while for birders and all those who had beautiful and strange birds in their yards, it will be that incredible day in May when birds dropped from the sky.

---

23 *MAY* 1997

The bird line registered over fifty calls and was filled with reports of Baltimore orioles, rose-breasted grosbeaks, cedar waxwings, indigo buntings, and ruby-throated hummingbirds. Several feeders had as many as six to eight orioles and four or more rose-breasted grosbeaks in attendance.

While there had been no real waves of migrant warblers this spring that changed dramatically on the rainy, foggy, drizzly morning of the 20th after intense thunderstorms the night before. Astute readers or those with excellent memories might remember that last spring the island experienced a remarkable fallout of migrants on the 19th. Then on the 20th was record-breaking heat with temperatures soaring into the nineties. Nothing so spectacular this year but a very respectable flight of birds was moving on the evening of the 19th and there were lots of warblers on the 20th.

On the 16th and 17th, in fierce winds, a group comprised of Arnold Brown, Susan Yurkus, Bill Loughran, Alice Mohrman, and this writer went on a twenty-four-hour birdathon. The event, run by Massachusetts Audubon as a fund-raiser, ran from 6 PM on the 16th through to 6 PM on the 17th. The idea is to split the state into sections and try to see as many different species as possible in the specified time frame.

Despite the strong winds, the group scoured the island and recorded 129 different species of birds. There were other groups out on the island representing different sanctuaries, but our team had the experience, firsthand knowledge, and drive to make us overwhelming favorites. Home field advantage, the home team. Highlights included a singing Brewer's blackbird out at Katama Farm on Friday evening. This western species is rare and has only been

recorded in spring once before in the state, Nantucket on
3 April 1978. The bird was seen by that island's grand
dame and reknowned bird bander Edith Andrews.

Other highlights included a rare spring western sandpiper, two white-rumped sandpipers, a red-necked grebe,
and a yellow-throated warbler all in Chilmark. That is the
third yellow-throated warbler sighting this spring, which
is amazing for this southern species. All the swallows were
seen, with a cliff swallow over Squibnocket, as well as
approximately twenty purple martins.

31 MAY 1996

The number of birds seen last week was off the charts,
so there really is nowhere to go but down a notch or two.
After the incredible wave of nocturnal migrants that
arrived on the morning of 19 May, the residual effect was
noticeable until the morning of the 22nd when seemingly
all the northbound migrants had winged north in the
night. There were so many birds around that a sort of
birder burnout was at work. It was time for the birds to
move on and return the island to more "normal" springtime conditions.

Memorial Day Weekend is traditionally a great time
for birds. The problem for most is finding time away
from house guests and familial obligations to get some
birding in. The bird line had some thirty calls and many
observers and many first-time callers were reporting
seeing the same unforgettable species: namely, scarlet

tanager, rose-breasted grosbeak, or Baltimore oriole etching an indelible picture in their minds.

The most unusual bird seen was a strikingly marked and unmistakable southern raptor that was seen by Phil Swift flying over the Oak Bluffs landfill at 10 AM on the morning of the 21st. This bird was on the tail end of the warm front that brought the incursion of land birds on the 19th and was still heading northeast probably continuing to the Outer Cape. The bird Phil saw was a swallow-tailed kite, one of the most graceful birds of prey in the world.

These amazing falconlike kites have a clean black-and-white appearance with a long scissor-tail. Unfortunately for birders, the bird continued on its way and was only seen by the lucky few. Kites are long-distance migrants that winter in South America and make their way north to breeding grounds from Florida to South Carolina. Rarely do they overshoot this far north and appear in Massachusetts. However, these birds are being seen almost every spring now somewhere in the state, usually on the Cape and islands, thanks to more increasingly interested and knowledgeable observers.

Northern gannets and sooty shearwaters have been regular along the south shore especially in rain, fog, or southerly winds. Jean Wexler from North Tisbury spotted a black-billed cuckoo on the 25th, which is the first cuckoo reported this year.

If you're going to the beach, please don't bring the dog, but if you do make sure it is on a leash. Plover chicks and adults are spooked and terrified by four-legged critters.

> "All they could see
> was sky, water, birds, light,
> and confluence. It was the
> whole morning world."
> —*Eudora Welty*

Summer

AFTER THE INTENSE ACTIVITY OF MAY, the birding of summer slows down. Migrant species have passed through, arrived at their destinations, and are busy perpetuating their species. On the Vineyard, birds of the woods and fields are in every stage of nesting. Many have already fledged a first brood of young and are working on a second. The beaches have baby piping plovers, oystercatchers, and least terns, still unable to fly.

Prolonged periods of precipitation, northeast storms, and hot dry conditions all greatly affect breeding success. Each and every type of weather has inherent difficulties. But the most important environmental element is an abundant supply of insects to feed the young. Their energy demands expand daily, almost exponentially, as the nestlings grow at staggering rates. As the young get bigger, both adult birds forage from before sunup until after sundown trying to feed the insatiable chicks.

Shorebirds whose young are precocial are the sole exceptions to this pattern. A baby robin or blue jay hatches naked of feathers and helpless in the nest, requiring constant protection, brooding, and feeding. Precocial shorebirds, on the other hand, hatch out of the egg and are up and running in a few minutes. A baby killdeer or piping plover is never fed by the adults. It finds its own food, snatching up minuscule insects on the sand or ground. These chicks are especially hard hit by prolonged storms and cold, rainy conditions when the insects vanish. The young soon starve. The adults stay nearby and protect the chicks from predators, and may even brood them in inclement weather (rain or sun), but the chicks never get a free meal.

American oystercatchers have a different strategy. When the downy young are hatched they are able to run about almost instantly like other shorebirds. But rather than adopting a laissez-faire attitude, adult oystercatchers have to be fierce in defense of their young or crows and gulls would gobble up the chicks in short order. The oystercatchers' beautiful orange beaks are not only good for shucking clams, but also good for pulling feathers out of the great black-backed gulls' heads, necks, and backs. And oystercatcher parenting extends further; because of the oystercatchers' unique diet of clams, steamers, quahogs, razorclams, and virtually any kind of shellfish they catch, the young need to be fed by the adults until they are taught how to open the shells.

As June turns to July, the first migrants on the southbound journey—sandpipers and plovers—begin to appear on island beaches and mudflats. These most mobile of all birds travel to the ends of the Earth, annually. Taking advantage of the round-the-clock daylight in extreme northern latitudes, they court, lay eggs, incubate, and hatch young in short order. Many adults have left their young on the tundra and returned here on the southbound journey, starting on the Fourth of July.

Every frontal system in July and August will carry birds south. Again, nasty weather is friend to the birder, particularly on the tidal flats where strong winds and rain may force the long-distance flier to rest. The uglier the weather, the better the birding. The Vineyard does not have great shorebird habitat. These tremendously strong flying birds stage at areas that have far greater food resources like Monomoy Point, Newburyport, or in the Bay of Fundy with its huge tides. But the beaches, tidal flats, and shorelines are certainly not devoid of birds in fine weather. There are lots of sandpipers, plovers, gulls, and flocks of resting terns.

By the end of July the first land birds have begun to migrate south: yellow warblers, northern waterthrushes, orioles, and blackbirds. August heralds the start of a major exodus, and the cold fronts with northwest winds of mid-month can carry many feathered travelers. By the end of August, migration has just about cranked up to full-bore, and the birding is exceptional.

For a birding junkie, hurricanes are storms that dreams are made of. Typhoons are just noisy disturbances in the Pacific—but hurricanes, bring on the big ones! While this may not be a sane reaction, it is the only one a true bird nut can manifest, because the birds swept in on the coat-tails of a summer or fall hurricane are unforgettable. But should you happen to be visiting our area and a hurricane is approaching, run for cover. There will be plenty to see once the monster has roared its last.

JUNE

"These are the days when Birds come back—/A very few—a Bird or two—/To take a backward look/These are the days when skies resume/The old—old sophistries of June—/A blue and gold mistake." —*Emily Dickinson*

BREED, BREED, BREED. In June, birds settle down to the serious task of chick raising. Spring migration is basically over. This is an excellent time of year for some far-ranging strays to appear but is generally fairly routine. It is a great time to learn the resident birds and to observe interesting behaviors associated with nesting and raising young.

Migrant warblers, particularly the most northerly nesters that breed on the taiga in the band of spruces running across the top of the continent, are among the last migrants to come through along with other boreal nesters and shorebirds that breed as far north as there is exposed land. These often are found into the first and occasionally second week of the month.

Although the summer is just beginning for the bipedal population, the birds are smack in the middle of their season. My bird hot line is abuzz with reports of birds falling out of nests, baby birds that can't fly, baby birds being spotted all over, in the likeliest and unlikeliest places. The most common question is "what should I do if I find a baby bird in trouble?" The only sensible course of action is to leave the bird alone and create as little disturbance as possible. Your intervention can't help. The cries you hear from these babies are normal. Fledglings call incessantly to their parents so that the adult birds can locate them when they return from a foraging trip.

If you find a young bird that appears abandoned, leave it alone. The adults are either watching over it or out searching for food. Try not to bring attention to the young bird, so as not to alert predators. The stress of being in contact with humans is enough to kill most birds. Their chances of survival are worse if you pick them up. The best chance they have is by staying where they are.

Leaving the nest is one of the most dangerous moments in a bird's life. All land birds grow quickly and develop flight feathers in about three to four weeks. Flying must be learned. Even though they are inherently perfect flying machines, they must still practice, practice, practice to master the technique.

The young leave the nest after two to three weeks, but are not able to fly effectively enough to escape predators for another few days. So-called branchers stay close to the nest on branches, hopefully out of harm's way. Their flying skills are shaky at best, they have no experience with predators, and they lack street smarts, to use a highly technical ornithological term. Fortunately, the adults stay with them, and in most cases continue to feed and attempt to protect them for some time. After a while, the young begin to supplement their meals when the adults are away.

Depending on the species, the adults quickly wean the young by reducing the food they bring. In some cases, the female lays another clutch of eggs when the young are fledged and she begins incubating while the male continues to feed the last batch of young. It is a difficult time for the "teenage" birds and they are apt to get into all kinds of mishaps, which can be extremely entertaining for the bird observer.

─────────

13 JUNE 1997

Finally, eight days before the summer solstice, the temperature has risen. We've gone from winter to summer in a seemingly miraculous span of about a week. The first week of June was abysmal with northeast winds and wind chills approaching winterlike numbers. On the morning of June 9th the temperature bottomed out at thirty-three degrees in the frost bottoms or cold sinks at the heads of the many coves of the Great Ponds in Edgartown and West Tisbury. By the time you read this, temperatures in the eighties should have occurred and optimistically summer will be here to stay.

The weather stayed cold for so long that an adult Mississippi kite that had been discovered in Orleans on the Cape was picked up dead on the morning of the 5th. These raptors feed almost exclusively on flying insects. With the prevailing northeast wind and cold temperatures, the bird could not find enough food. There were no large insects moving either in the air or on the ground.

You can say that the weather killed this bird, which is why these kites don't live in New England. They are tropical birds that are only in North America for a few summer months, then fly back to the tropics.

While it is almost the middle of June and migration is over for the time being, some migrants were stranded here as a result of the strange cold weather. The morning of the 6th brought some surprises: in the campground and near the cemetery in Oak Bluffs were singing warblers, six blackpolls, and three Canadas. Susan Yurkus and Jay Eliasberg were out birding at the pumping station in Oak Bluffs and heard a blackpoll giving its full song—a first for the island. These birds certainly did not arrive on the northeast wind from Georges Bank but most likely arrived a week to ten days earlier and then got pinned down by the inclement weather and unfavorable winds. Unable and unwilling to fly into a stiff and cold headwind, the birds were forced to remain on the island much longer than the one day they had intended. The last lingering blackpoll warbler cleared out on the night of the 9th on the warm southwest wind that arrived.

Black-billed cuckoos have been widespread the past week or so. The cuckoos that occur on the Vineyard include the black-billed and its close relation, the yellow-billed cuckoo. The cuckoos are quiet, shy birds that usually remain hidden and quite still in the foliage of trees and shrubs. In hot weather, especially humid summer days, cuckoos will call. They also call while flying, or sitting on the nest. You can often hear them high overhead at night. The calls are loud and distinctive.

Black-billeds give a series of "cu-cu-cu-cu-cu" all on the same low pitch. Yellow-billeds have more variation, making sounds like "kow-kow-keow-kow" and then ending with a slowed down "kowk-kowk."

Armed with these helpful descriptions, you will now promptly hear and recognize calling cuckoos. Pay attention to the sound in the middle of a sticky day—nothing else is singing. Nancy Rogers from Vineyard Haven had a black-billed cuckoo collide with her window on the 9th. The bird did not survive but Nancy got excellent looks at it and was able to get a crash course (pun intended) in cuckoo identification. The two species that occur here (there are 127 species worldwide) are quite alike but, with a little practice, easily distinguishable.

A pair of warbling vireos has taken up residence at the head of the lagoon in Oak Bluffs. They have been there for over a month. These drab nondescript vireos are scarce on the Vineyard and have never been known to breed. The pair in Oak Bluffs has been observed gathering nesting material and the male sings almost all day long. This is the island's first nesting pair.

19 JUNE 1998

After experiencing a spring that bordered on idyllic, with what I imagine to be typical Southern California weather, it all came to an end on the last full weekend of spring. When it rained—it poured. The entire New England region was inundated. There were record-breaking amounts of rainfall. Boston suffered major flooding damage. The mayor was calling for federal disaster relief.

It was the heaviest and hardest rainfall that I have ever seen on Martha's Vineyard in twenty years, except in a hurricane. It was really bad news for breeding birds—the disaster of '98.

Sunday is the longest day of the year, the start of summer in the Northern Hemisphere. Breeding birds know this instinctively and have timed their breeding cycle to coincide with this period of maximum daylight and food availability. This is why virtually all birds present on the island now either have eggs of a second brood, nestlings that are being fed, or newly fledged young.

Unfortunately, after the extraordinarily heavy rains accompanied by strong winds and thunder and lightning, many birds have lost their nests or nestlings and are either finished for the season or starting over. Many species of neotropical migrants only have time for one nesting in a season and the loss of eggs or young represents a complete loss for this year. The extent of the damage and loss is still not fully determined but judging from phone reports and what I have seen—mortality rates are high.

Aside from the actual water falling, the biggest problem for an adult bird is how to secure food. Virtually all baby land birds are fed protein-rich insects as nestlings and after fledging. A long nasty, rainy, windy weekend like this one causes insects to seek cover and prevents the hatching or emerging of new bugs. So what the day before was an abundant food supply with insects ripe for the picking, as it were, becomes an empty cupboard. If the weather is sufficiently horrible, it forces one adult to stay and physically brood or shelter the young in an attempt to keep them warm and dry.

This is a double whammy as it prevents that bird from looking for and providing much needed food and if the young are even half-grown they all cannot possibly fit beneath the adult. Depending on the growth of the brood and nest position, many birds get wet and because they are not yet fully feathered, quickly freeze. If they don't freeze, starvation claims them. It was a very bad weekend for native bird life.

Fortunately, not all birds had trouble and the ones that survived the tempest will have a great abundance of food because of all the rainfall stimulating the rapidly growing vegetation that will, in turn, provide food for innumerable insects. A willet has been seen repeatedly over many weeks along the Beach Road in Edgartown. While a common breeder in all the salt marshes on the Cape, they are still scarce on the Vineyard.

Paul Jackson, aka bluebird man, reports that his son watched a really beautiful thing in West Tisbury. He saw a mix and match of shocking blues, with smaller amounts of orange and brown, fluttering around like blue leaves all over in the trees, on the grass, accompanied by the most lovely sounds. Across from the main airport, south

towards Long Point Refuge, his son had just mowed a
field. The next day a flock of thirty-five to forty eastern
bluebirds descended on the field to partake of the available insects, grasshoppers, and the like that had been
exposed by the mowing. This is unusual at this season but
bluebirds are gregarious and normally travel in flocks of
varying sizes most of the year. This was undoubtably several family groups that had nested nearby and were quick
to partake of the feast.

The stormy weather did bring some pelagic birds
within view of the south side of the island if you could see
through all the rain. Most birds that were identifiable were
sooty shearwaters, but there were also a couple of greater
and a few manx shearwaters seen as well.

23 *JUNE* 1995

The first serious heat has arrived with the first week of
summer. South of the equator, this week contained the
shortest day of the year. From sixty-six degrees, thirty-
three minutes latitude, all the way to the South Pole
at ninety degrees south latitude, the 21st marks the mid-
point of six months of total polar darkness with astoundingly cold temperatures and the roaring winds of the
polar vortex.

Incredibly, there is a bird breeding with its kin, through
the Antarctic winter, standing, huddling en masse, on an
ice shelf near the base of a cliff, incubating a single egg.
The bird is kept on its feet covered by flaps of skin and

feathers. It is the largest penguin on Earth, the emperor penguin.

With the increased daylight back in our own hemisphere, the Arctic begins its brief, but rich summer. The diversity of flowers and insects, and the incredible abundance of food, while only for a short while, makes an ideal habitat for nesting sandpipers and plovers. They arrive on breeding grounds in early to mid-June, and their stay is brief.

Which raises the question of what three white-rumped sandpipers were doing on the flats at Katama on the 15th and a seemingly paired couple still there on the 17th. These birds may still "blast off" for the tundra, which is a minimum of a thousand miles north, and breed this year. This species flies impressively and could be on breeding territory in two days, lay eggs a few days after, and have hatchlings in less than three weeks.

Some surprising birds were reported this past week. Highlights include an adult yellow-crowned night heron seen feeding along the shore of a freshwater pond at dawn on the morning of the 15th. This seldom seen, secretive night heron reaches the extreme northern edge of its range in Massachusetts and is always scarce on the Vineyard. There have been reports of adult yellow-crowns a few times this season along the shores of Sengekontacket and a pair is probably nesting somewhere in Edgartown.

Hollis Smith was fishing at dusk and came across an injured tubenose on the beach. Tubenoses are seabirds that have what looks like small double-barreled shotguns mounted on top of their beaks. The strange apparatus is part of a specialized desalinization system that enables them to drink salt water. The very concentrated brine drips out of the tubes onto the bill. Not recognizing this odd bird immediately, Hollis noted the field marks and looked it up in his bird book when he got home. He had seen an adult, white morph, northern fulmar, a gull-like tubenose—of the shearwater family—that is rare off Vineyard shores. The bird had a bad leg injury but did not stay around and hopefully returned to open ocean where it lives.

27 JUNE 1997

School is out, the temperature is up, and people are heading in droves for the cooling influence of the coastline. Crowds are arriving on island shores. It is summer on the Vineyard.

Virtually all species of land birds that are here now are breeding birds. Most of the birds along the shorelines and flying to and fro are nesting. Least terns and piping plovers are feeding and guarding chicks and dazzling colored American oystercatchers have large young.

The most noteworthy occurrence this past week was the discovery of an Acadian flycatcher singing and undoubtably breeding in a wooded swamp in Gay Head or Aquinnah. Leah Tofte-Dorr and I located the singing bird on the morning of the 23rd in an extremely dense

concentration of mosquitoes, poison ivy, and both deer
and wood ticks. A blue jay skulked in from nearby, setting
up a state of panic in the small flycatcher. It gave an alarm
call and attempted to distract the jay.

Jays at this season are notorious nest robbers, eating
either eggs or young, and this flycatcher was not at all
fooled by the jay's quiet demeanor. The flycatcher kept
up the alarm until the jay moved off. It then flew off a
short distance but did not start calling again. By the bird's
agitated behavior and obvious discomfort with the jay,
it seems apparent that the bird had a nest nearby. This
southern flycatcher has been slowly extending its range
northward and reaches its northern limit in Massachusetts. This is a welcome addition to the island's avifauna.

28 JUNE 1996

The island's biomass, the weight of living organisms present, increases exponentially in the summer months. The
human population increases most dramatically and affects
all other life-forms. Most roadways are clogged with cars,
buses, and bicycles. Not only is the human population
soaring, but native animals from butterflies, moths, and
dragonflies, to mice, squirrels, rabbits, otters, and deer are
hard at work raising new members of whatever species
they might be, swelling their population numbers.

The warm temperatures and benign weather along
with an abundance of plant and insect food make this the
time to replicate the species. Many of our more common
birds will lay two, or rarely three, and even four clutches

of eggs in a season that begins in April and ends in late
August or even September.

If all goes well and food is abundant, bird life can really
crank out some numbers. A pair of robins, for example,
can begin breeding in early April and have young hatching
by about the third week. When the young are out of the
nest, the male will continue to feed them for a while but
the female will begin building another nest and commence
egg laying shortly thereafter. If the nest is able to avoid de-
tection by predators, they will continue to breed right
though the summer. With sets of four eggs/young in each
nest, a pair of robins with three broods could raise twelve
new robins or four broods, sixteen robins in one season.

Birds are extremely vulnerable during the breeding
season as these most mobile of animals are tied to the
nest. Predators ranging from snakes, squirrels, raccoons,
skunks, and other birds love to eat eggs, young, and even
the adults if they can catch them. But many species have a
longer incubation and short nestling period. A failed or
robbed nest spells disaster for the whole season. As long
as the adult escapes, it will nest another season.

Stan Panitz of Chilmark has a wood duck family using
an owl box to nest. The box has been up for three years
and this year a pair of wood ducks is raising a family with
no water in sight. These stunningly beautiful ducks are
secretive around nesting holes and easy to pass by. They
are remarkable, but it seems shocking to see a duck coming out of a box in the woods, high up in a tree, with no
water nearby. Don Sibley called from West Tisbury to

report a male indigo bunting that appeared at his feeder on the 21st. This species has never been known to breed on the Vineyard but certainly seems like it should. The habitat along the north side is ideal, but as yet they have never been even suspected of nesting.

JULY

"Now the summer came to pass / And flowers through the grass / Joyously sprang / While all the tribes of birds sang."
— *Walther von der Vogelweide*

THE MONTH THAT STARTS with exuberant fireworks marks the end of the prodigious bird song of May and June. Birds on the island are just finishing raising a family. The pace of a bird's life makes our existence seem to be moving in slow motion. Birds maintain a nearly constant, frenetic, athletic level of activity, with some of the highest metabolic rates and body temperatures of any living creature.

It's time for the young to get out on their own. Mortality is highest at this point in a bird's life. The young creatures must learn to recognize predators and other threats, master the skills of flying, find food and water, and shortly undertake a long-distance migration based solely on instinctive information. Good luck.

The hardest work of fledgling rearing is just ending and now is the time to bask in the warmth and take advantage of the food. The adults are growing new feathers to replace the worn ones in preparation for the trip south. Most species do this refurbishing over a four- to six-week period at the end of the breeding season. The molt coincides with the storing up of fat for the upcoming migration.

Bird migration is in partial swing and particularly noticeable along the shores, sandbars, mudflats, and waters surrounding the Vineyard. The plovers and sandpipers that call both hemispheres home are stopping here for a few hours to a few weeks.

These birds have a variation on the typical breeding strategy. After the young hatch, the adults stay with them for ten days or so before saying *hasta la vista* and heading south. *Vaya con dios*, little ones, you're on your own. Obviously proponents of the empty nest syndrome.

Back from the shoreline—granted it's no day at the beach—many bird species are beginning to gather and travel about woodlands in mixed flocks. There are many family groups with newly fledged young who are making a racket as they beg for food from the increasingly unresponsive adults. The problem for birders is that biting insects are as thick as they ever get on the island. The mosquitos, deer flies, green head flies, and gnats or no-see-ums, not to mention deer ticks, can make it challenging to hold a pair of binoculars steady. Invest in your favorite insect repellant.

Gulls and terns are also finished with nesting. An intimidating number of gulls are now patrolling the crowded beaches. Both herring and great black-backed gulls, now freed from parental responsibilities, look upon the people on the beach as a fast-food drive-up window. They are amazingly bold—while not exactly nest robbing, they have figured out that any unattended bag, blanket, or cooler is fair game. With their powerful bills, they can destroy things very quickly. By July their smaller and much quicker cousin, the ring-billed gull, arrives from inland breeding grounds around the Great Lakes and travels in kleptoparasitical flocks of ten to twenty. They are even faster and sneakier than their larger cousins.

Terns are also finished nesting and flocks of them are increasing in the abundantly well-stocked waters around the island. Many breed on nearby islands in Buzzard's Bay or around Cape Cod. When the young fledge, the adults head straight for the island with the young winging behind. They are still totally dependent on their parents for food and need to fatten for the fall migration. Many bird species exhibit what is called post-breeding dispersal—after nesting, they wander widely. Southern species head north and vice versa.

---

1 *JULY* 1994

The big bird news is about a new bird for Massachusetts. This means that in the long tradition and excellent coverage in one of the oldest and most heavily birded states, a bird that has never been seen before has appeared and been well documented on full frame videotape. Even better the bird has hung around for a little while, allowing a small army of observers to see it. Many people came from all over New England and farther to attempt to view the first snowy plover in the state's history. The snowy plover is a small bird that is remarkably similar to the endangered piping plover. It is slightly smaller with minor plumage differences and black legs and beak, as opposed to the piper's orange legs and beak.

This plover had never turned up anywhere north of the Carolinas. Its North American range is along the shores of the Gulf of Mexico west to the Pacific Coast. It was discovered because of the protection being afforded its close relative, the piping plover. Shorebird monitors checking on plover nests first saw the bird.

Realizing the rarity of the snowy plover and similarity between the cousins, they were cautious in the identification. The bird was first seen on 11 June at Sea Gull Beach in Yarmouth. Subsequently, it was seen on an island in Chatham to the east and New Seabury to the west. This bird has wings and used them. Finally the bird reappeared at Sea Gull beach on the afternoon of the 23rd and the hot line kicked in, letting the bird out of the bag so to speak.

The bird stayed on this beach until dark and was found again the next morning. Not to waste this opportunity, Arnold Brown and this writer departed that afternoon for "the bird." Alas, because of the intense use of the beach on a Friday afternoon there was no snowy plover.

At six the next morning in dense fog, there were already a hundred birders stalking the tiny plover. Amazingly, the bird showed up a little after seven and was not at all concerned with the human presence. The state's already impressive bird list has just grown by one more.

Back on the Vineyard, bald eagles continue to impress. Andy Goldman was out fishing with Scott McDowell on the *Bass n Blue* on the 22nd near Squibnocket. Looking towards the beach, they saw a huge dark bird. Going in for a closer look, they saw a bald eagle eating a rabbit. They also saw a sooty shearwater flying near No Man's Land.

Gus Ben David had quite a start the other day as he heard a loud crash against his door. Quickly running over to see the cause of the commotion, he saw one of his pigeons, a white king, stunned at the door. In the same instant, an adult Cooper's hawk was on the bird and Gus went flying out the door, so to speak, startling the hawk into dropping his bird.

4 *JULY 1997*

The official start of the summer season has arrived seemingly in the blink of an eye. After a lingering, cold spring that felt like winter with people wearing parkas to the beach only three weeks ago, the summer weather makes that time a more distant memory than the calendar suggests.

Many species have already raised their first brood and are working on number two. Some species may raise three full broods in one season, for example American robins, eastern bluebirds, and Carolina wrens, while most others manage only one or occasionally two.

For each species every season is different with many factors responsible for breeding success, along with a bit of luck. The amount of rainfall is critical: too much causes problems, just as too little prevents plant and insect development from peaking at the right time for insectivorous birds. This year's breeding season has been excellent for Vineyard birds as the weather and the temperature responded when the birds had very hungry young. A three-day spell of northeast winds and rain in June or early July causes certain havoc and chick mortality in many species. Fish-eating species are very hard-pressed when high winds and rain cause turbulent dirty water, and runoff makes the water murky and the small fish they require invisible.

Debra Swanson and daughter Emma were on a stake-out of a threatened Vineyard breeding bird, the northern harrier, up on Moshup's Trail in Gay Head. They arrived at dawn and sat in an innocuous way, Debra watching, Emma sleeping, hoping to catch a glimpse of the male arriving with food and calling to the female, who flies up to meet him so they can execute a food pass.

She then proceeds in a sneaky way back to the nest, so that even watchful humans will be confounded about the exact whereabouts of the nest. While the harriers did not cooperate this morning, a calling willow flycatcher did. This is a small, greenish flycatcher in the exceedingly difficult genus *Empidonax*. The genus basically can only be identified when the male is calling on territory, like this male was doing right along Moshup's Trail. This is a new breeding record for this species in the town of Gay Head.

Another hard-to-locate breeding species that fluctuates from zero to several pairs annually is the orchard oriole. This smaller relative of the Baltimore oriole has a fondness for fruit trees, hence its common name. On the 25th, Leah Tofte-Dorr located a male singing in a residential area abutting the state forest in West Tisbury.

Some rather unusual species have arrived from points south with all the beautiful weather the past couple of weeks. Royal terns, a large saltwater species that is common from New Jersey south in the breeding season but rare north of Long Island, have appeared. They are scarce but occur fairly regularly along Vineyard shores in very small numbers most years. They were nonexistent last season but things appear heading in a different direction for this summer. On the 24th a single bird was seen by Charlie Morano in Edgartown Harbor in the late afternoon and another, possibly the same individual, was seen flying over the drawbridge between Oak Bluffs and Vineyard Haven at 11 AM that morning. Allan Keith found a single bird on Sarson's Island on the 28th and Gus Daniels located it again on the 29th. Four sightings of royal terns on the island in June is significant and their numbers will probably increase during the next month. It is not possible to confirm that this was four different birds, although this writer thinks so.

Lou Hathaway had quite a sight on the evening of the 27th as a pair of black skimmers flew by him at the big bridge dividing Edgartown and Oak Bluffs. These bizarre birds, the only birds in the world with elongated lower mandibles, are strikingly colored and fly magnificently. A tropical species, they reach their extreme northern limit in Massachusetts in summer, occasionally staying to breed on the Cape and islands or in Plymouth. They have bright orange bills and look like some sort of seagoing toucans that escaped from the zoo. Last, Richard Greene had good views of a small buteo, a broad-winged hawk. This woodland species, common over most of eastern North America, is not known to breed on the island but perhaps it may be a subadult summering. Either way it is very interesting.

7 JULY 1995

The crush of humanity that arrived on the island for the Fourth of July was incredible. When the Mormons were saved from the locust plague by the return of the ravenous California gulls, it meant they would not starve from crop failure. For the island economy, geared for the seasonal boom, we hope it means something similar.

With the perfect weather for beach and boating, there were no remote spots on the Vineyard. There were more people than birds on every beach. But right on schedule from breeding areas well to the north on the tundra and muskeg arrived the first southbound shorebirds. Having just fulfilled their strident need to reproduce their species, they next look after themselves. Feeding and resting are important after all the wear and tear of nesting. They also must replace all their feathers.

Every species' timetable and distance-to-be-covered is variable. In fact individuals of the same species may winter from Cape Cod, Massachusetts to the southern tip of South America, the most elongated of any wintering range. That is exactly what the small sandpiper that runs along at the edge of the surf, the sanderling, does.

Birding this time of year is a bit slow with the heat, the end of the nesting season, the deer flies, and the summer crowds. Remarkably, in the birds-have-wings-and-they-use-them category, a bird that has only been seen once before on the Atlantic Coast of North America, and only four times in North America period, has miraculously appeared not far from the Vineyard. On a clear day from the Gay Head Cliffs looking due west one can see the supports for the Newport, Rhode Island bridge. A few miles north of there, near the Newport/Middletown line, is this rare bird.

Of the approximately forty-seven species of gulls in the world, this is not one that I would expect in eastern North America. Its range is Asiatic. It breeds on the coasts and islands in eastern Siberia, Korea, northern China, and both islands of Japan. In winter it disperses north to Sakhalin and south to Hong Kong. There are no similar birds that resemble its range. It is a medium-sized gull, dark-backed, with a yellow bill with a black band and a red tip: the black-tailed gull.

Susan Yurkus, Allan Keith, and Paul Miliotis were out birding and looking for butterflies over the past week and found some unusual things. Then on the 4th near the

Tisbury/West Tisbury line they found a small colony of Baltimore checker-spot butterflies. This beautiful medium-sized, black, orange, and white butterfly had not been seen by any of them on the Vineyard before.

14 JULY 1995

Summer is here, in full force. The island is swarming with people and it seems in danger of sinking into the surrounding waters, under the awesome weight and sheer numbers of humanity packed into such a finite space. For birds, the annual cycle has already swung to fall. Redwinged blackbirds, common grackles, and cowbirds can be seen flying off to roost in small flocks at dusk. And just a short while ago the blackbirds were defending territories from each other!

Colonial nesting terns have fledged young and moved away from nesting colonies closer to the most productive fishing grounds. These most graceful of birds feed exclusively on small live fish that they catch by diving headfirst into the water, plunge-diving. A young tern must not only learn how to fly quickly and strongly, but then how to dive headfirst into the water and catch small fish. Learning to fish this way is a very difficult skill and it takes a long time before a young tern can fish well enough to feed itself. Consequently, the adults stay with the young for the fall migration and into their first winter, feeding them the entire time.

Terns have been studied intensively for over fifty years.

Because they nest in dense, tightly packed colonies and return to the same colony to breed each year, they are ideal subjects for research. By banding tern chicks just before they are capable of flight, they can be captured and banded without undue disturbance or harm. The bands are all numbered and often color bands are added so individual birds can be identified in binoculars without recapturing. It has been found that the older a tern is the more successful it becomes at rearing chicks. They are more knowledgeable about where to fish in inclement weather when starvation of young chicks is the biggest cause of mortality.

A bird that has been suspected of breeding on the island for the past five years has finally been confirmed. Cooper's hawks are crow-sized, powerful hawks that have relatively short wings and long tails. They are in the genus *Accipiter*, one of three species in North America. They feed heavily on birds that they capture on the wing. For several summers these birds have been seen flying along at various island locales sometimes carrying a dead bird in their talons, presumably heading for a nest.

They are very secretive and pick quiet heavily wooded areas with no human disturbance to nest in. All hawks are individuals at the nest site; some will attack intruders, while others will skulk away never to be discovered. The largest accipiter, the goshawk, is famous for defending its nest. Intruders are attacked at eye level by these ferocious birds uttering a bloodcurdling scream. They have opened up heads with their talons. Going near a goshawk nest requires the use of a steel helmet or serious hard hat. Cooper's hawks may or may not defend the nest and attack intruders.

Bob Shriber was searching for the Acadian flycatcher that has been a fixture calling in the woods at Waskosim's Rock. While out on the morning of the 7th he did not find the flycatcher but got the attention of a female Cooper's hawk and came under heavy attack by the calling and very mad female. He spotted the nest and quickly vacated the area as getting attacked by a large accipiter is much different from hearing the call of a small flycatcher. While not able to tell if young were in the nest, as it was fifty or sixty feet up in a tree, he thinks it is safe to assume from the bird's behavior that nestlings are in the nest or recently fledged young are nearby.

Another probable first nesting for a bird on the Vineyard is a shorebird called a willet. These salt marsh-loving sandpipers are big and noisy. They commonly nest in salt marshes all over Cape Cod and are abundant on North Monomoy Island. The Vineyard just did not have enough salt marsh to attract nesting willets but for the past few years there have been willets around Pocha Pond on Chappaquiddick all summer. On the Beach Road, in the marsh near the bend in the road, has been a couple of very noisy, aggressive, and territorial willets. No nest has been found but it seems from the birds' actions that young may be in the *Spartina* grass.

19 JULY 1996

Tropical Storm Bertha passed by the Vineyard on the afternoon and early evening of the 13th. The former hurricane had lost most of its zip and for residents used to big blows and nor'easters it was a big zero. Alas, visions of tropical terns, pelicans, and frigate birds were put on hold.

Fortunately, many birders were excited at the prospects of what may have been driven north by the massive storm system that slammed into the Carolinas and had been very strong over much of the eastern Caribbean for many days. George "Gus" Daniels and Allan Keith birded their way up and down Chappaquiddick, as they have virtually every weekend since April, to census the shorebird numbers. Standing on the bluff near the Cape Pogue lighthouse, they saw a remarkable bird fly by. Both are expert observers with experience all over the world. They found a bird that has never been seen before on the Vineyard, in the state of Massachusetts, indeed anywhere in eastern North America. When and if the identification is fully agreed upon, it will, in all likelihood, be a new North American record.

The bird was initally identified by Allan Keith as the West Indian race of the black swift, *Cypsoloides niger*. Other observers fortunate to see this bird were Peter Alden, Bill Loughran, Arnold and Edie Brown, Janice Callaghan, and Lanny McDowell. This writer saw the bird twice that day for an hour and a half at noon, then again with the aforementioned group for an hour, and watched it go roost on the Cape Pogue lighthouse. Peter Alden began declaring it an *Apus apus*, the European swift, immediately upon seeing it. This is the only swift known to commonly roost on man-made structures. We respectfully agree to disagree on the bird's identity. It looked like a large purple martin with a long deeply forked tail and the wings of a swift. This writer hopes that both the West Indian black swift and the European swift will colonize the Vineyard in huge numbers and eat all the obnoxious mosquitoes and green headed flies.

In other bird news, things are starting to pick up on the beaches and tidal flats. Southbound migrating sandpipers and plovers are appearing in good numbers. Large flocks of terns that have just moved away from nesting islands in Nantucket Sound, on the Cape, in Buzzard's Bay, and from other outlying areas are beginning to show up on Vineyard beaches. The waters surrounding the island are loaded with small sand eels and other fish that attract terns and many species of game fish. When the terns fledge their chicks, they move to Vineyard beaches to rest and feed themselves and their now flying young.

Roseate terns, one of the rarest tern species in the world, become common in Menemsha Basin and along the shores of Edgartown from now until the end of August.

Often the young birds will sit on a convenient sandbar and form flocks while the adult is out fishing. The flocks of terns tend to congregate at the same place at certain tides. Once these spots are identified, they are worth checking frequently as groups of terns attract other terns and small gulls. Many an unusual species has been found hanging out with flocks of terns.

In the aftermath of Tropical Storm Bertha, another group of birders walked down Norton's Point, the spit of land that connects the big island to Chappaquiddick, at dawn to look at what the storm may have brought. While not encountering any tropical species, the group had fabulous looks at many shorebird species.

Jeff Verner, Jerry McCarthy, Lanny McDowell, and this writer were scoping off south beach at 5 AM but did not see any pelagic species. On the trip down the beach, we were rewarded with good numbers of shorebirds, including a lone Wilson's phalarope. This is the first phalarope reported in a couple of years.

AUGUST

"We're never single-minded, unperplexed, like migratory birds."
—*Rainer Maria Rilke*

THE DOG DAYS OF AUGUST see the fall migration get underway in full force. The next few months on the Vineyard offer some of the finest birding in the country and among the best in New England. From the cliffs at Gay Head to the beaches on Chappaquiddick, the island offers a chance to see concentrations of migrants in an uncrowded, relaxed atmosphere. The best land birding is to be had in the morning, the earlier the better. Any of the MV land bank properties or the state forest offer good places to find migrant and resident species.

The days are getting noticeably shorter and the time before many species must head south is only a few short weeks away. The woods and fields are quiet now — the decreased levels of bird song indicate a concentration on eating as much as possible. Most birds are also engaged in the annual business of growing a new set of feathers, an energy-draining proposition.

Cool evening temperatures and light northwest winds bring a taste of the fall. The tiny insectivorous land birds do not linger for long after raising their young, so they begin to head south by early to mid-August. Flocks of migrant warblers come in on weak cold fronts with northwest winds anytime after midmonth, as do flycatchers.

In fact the end of this month and the beginning of the next, Labor Day weekend in particular, are the best times of year for seeing the greatest number and greatest diversity of warblers and vireos. At night and early in the morning migrants can already be heard overhead. Yellow warblers, redstarts, and northern waterthrushes depart early and can be found at land bird traps already.

Sandpipers and plovers are finished nesting and are cruising on south at a leisurely pace. Some stop to rest and feed on Vineyard shores. Any tidal flat will have some birds but the flats at Norton's Point consistently have the most birds. Any of the openings of the Great Ponds can be very good if the ponds are open, the water low, and there are exposed flats and sandbars for the birds to rest and feed on.

Many immature birds will not survive their first full year. The rigors of life in the wild are demanding and mistakes are not forgiven. A simple error in any of the routine activities can spell disaster. Most birds undertake perilous migrations with no guides, maps, or experience—it is a wonder that any survive. But survive and thrive they do, with knowledge honed by millions of years of survivors.

2 AUGUST 1996

August is here and the birding is improving daily. From now until mid-October, the waters surrounding the Vineyard will be teeming with marine life, particularly an abundance of small bait fishes. Sand eels and silverside minnows provide the food for virtually all the game fish and many birds. The beaches, sandbars, and mudflats around the island are playing host to large numbers of terns right now. The birds have left breeding colonies and are staging on Vineyard shores before heading south for the winter.

One of the Vineyard specialties is the roseate tern. Roseate terns were listed as endangered by the United States Fish and Wildlife Service in 1987 because the population had become dangerously concentrated into a few colony sites. In Massachusetts and elsewhere, the birds were displaced from offshore islands to inshore sites by nesting herring and great black-backed gulls. The predation on inshore areas from mammals (raccoons and skunks), great horned owls, and black-crowned night herons was and continues to be catastrophic.

Over in Buzzard's Bay is a small island called Bird Island, not far offshore in the town of Marion, Massachusetts. It is the only site in Massachusetts where the terns have been relatively secure from significant predation and it now supports about half the entire population of the species in North America. Great Gull Island, off New York's Long Island, supports the other half of the population with many small exploratory colonies attempting to breed in other islets off New England locations. Roseate terns are a rare bird almost everywhere and birders find it one of the Vineyard's rewards to be able to observe good numbers easily and learn how to separate this species from its more common relatives.

The first reported upland sandpiper of the season was discovered by Janice Lynn Callaghan at dusk on the 29th at Katama. These lovely shorebirds are extreme long-distance migrants and their appearance is an event that signifies the real start of the fall migration.

Allan Keith and Gus Daniels birded the outer beach on Chappaquiddick down to the Cape Pogue Gut on the 27th and had an immature little blue heron, a black tern along with about three hundred commons and roseates, and a migrant orchard oriole out near the lighthouse. The orchard oriole is always a rare bird on the island after mid-June and is one of the earliest land bird migrants to depart south. They are scarce in their southbound travels and are rarely seen, particularly on the Vineyard.

In Memoriam
Roger Tory Peterson

The most famous naturalist in the United States and the man responsible for millions of people's interest in birds and other wildlife passed away on the 28th of July 1996, peacefully in his sleep. He was a remarkable fellow, whose paintings with key field marks pointed out enabled amateurs to identify all sorts of animals, plants, and fungi that had previously been accessible to only a few scientists and students. His first *Field Guide to the Birds* was published in 1934 by risk-taking Houghton Mifflin and revolutionized the way Americans learned to identify birds and eventually all wildlife.

He became as close to royalty as one can get in this country. He was awarded the presidential Medal of Freedom by President Carter, which is a nonmilitary award much like being knighted in the United Kingdom. He was awarded twenty-three honorary degrees. Aside from writing and illustrating a number of his own titles, he became the editor for the entire Peterson field guide series. Hardly a household can be found that does not have at least one Peterson guide in its library.

He had many close friends on the Vineyard. The late Guy Emerson, a famous ornithologist and formerly a summer resident of Chilmark, used to have Roger as a houseguest. Richard Pough, a longtime seasonal resident of Chilmark and author of the Audubon bird guides, has known Roger as a close friend for a lifetime. Roger was very close to the late Julian Hill, survived by his wife, the delightful Polly Hill, of West Tisbury. Roger attended many parties at the Hill's.

The late Edward Chalif, who had a summer residence at Abel's Hill in Chilmark, had a long association with Roger. Eddie, the entertaining ballet instructor, was locally famous for his Chilmark Community Center bird walks that were so popular despite the fact that birds were hard to find and see, but a good time was had by all. Eventually Roger and Eddie collaborated on *A Field Guide to Mexican Birds*, with the text done by Eddie and the paintings done by Roger. It was the first time all the tremendous bird life of that country had been illustrated.

While Roger's eyesight waned in his later years, his hearing was always fantastic. He could audio more birds than anyone in North America. He was the standard younger birders emulated. He taught school in Brookline and had Elliot Richardson as a student. He inspired Richardson, who went on to be an excellent birder in addition to holding positions in the cabinet under a couple of presidents.

This writer met Roger many times. Among the most memorable was when a new bird for North America showed up on Nantucket. A Western reef heron, one of the African herons, appeared at Quaise Marsh and caused a big stir in the bird world. Roger, Robert Ridgely, and Peter Alden chartered a plane from Groton, Connecticut (near the Peterson home in Old Lyme) and flew to Nantucket where this writer met them in a borrowed and battered land rover to get them to the marsh. We located the bird and then had lunch before they returned to the airport and flew off. All my exchanges with him will be lasting memories. He was a man who changed the world of naturalists.

---

4 *AUGUST 1995*

After seemingly endless weeks of hot weather, it's beginning to feel normal. Water temperatures are astoundingly high in area waters. Just ten miles south of the island, there is a warm eddy that shot off of the Gulf Stream bringing the temperature past eighty degrees Fahrenheit. With these kinds of temperatures, it's not surprising that many warm water fish have appeared close to shore. Yellowfin tuna and ballyhoo, small bait fish that resemble little billfish, are in the waters off Wasque.

What does water temperature have to do with birds, you ask. Cape Cod is a remarkable geographic barrier, primarily for its dividing effect on maritime currents. North of Cape Cod, cold water from the Gulf of Maine and the Bay of Fundy is stopped in Cape Cod Bay and heads east where it mixes with warmer southern currents and the Gulf Stream along the edge of the continental shelf and Georges Banks. Many pelagic bird species are associated with this colder, more oxygen-rich water.

South of Cape Cod are Martha's Vineyard and Nantucket separated from the Cape by two very shallow areas known as Vineyard and Nantucket Sounds, respectively. Tides are huge on the north side of the Cape, averaging about twelve feet, and much larger still to the north in the Bay of Fundy, averaging twenty-four feet. On the south side and the islands, they are only around three feet. Water in the sounds is like water in a bathtub, in comparison to north of Cape Cod, and it heats up dramatically. Many species of semitropical fish have appeared in Nantucket Sound that are not usually found north of the Carolinas. But normally the open ocean, Gulf Stream-roaming big game fish stay south and east of us to about the hundred fathom line. That is almost one hundred miles from land.

Many bird species are associated with warm water and open ocean conditions and are often found along this same hundred fathom line. Only in very recent years have pelagic birding trips been organized to get out to this area, which involves a rather lengthy sea trip and overnight on board. But virtually any pelagic bird that lives in the Caribbean or Sargasso Seas could and does appear off our shores when conditions and water temperatures are right. That is a very big reason to get excited about all this heat and what it's doing to water temperatures and the marine life.

Closer to shore things have been heating up as well. The prohibition of vehicle traffic on much of Norton's Point has allowed the formation of a salt marsh. High tide grass has taken root along the tide line and the first fiddler crabs have established themselves. Shorebirds in numbers never seen before on the island have found the undisturbed shores very welcoming. Numbers approaching a thousand or more are now found resting, sleeping, and preening along the shore at high tide.

Ruddy turnstones, semipalmated plovers, sanderlings, semipalmated and least sandpipers, and lesser numbers of many species can all be found enjoying the undisturbed north side of the dune line at high tide. When the tide is lower the birds are utilizing the vast amount of invertebrate food that lives in the rich organic ooze of a young salt marsh. Nesting oystercatchers and piping plovers, along with migrant greater yellowlegs and black-bellied plovers are very much in evidence.

Terns are very hard to miss right now. The rare southern royal tern has been sighted with regularity since the middle of May and could well be attempting to extend its breeding range. These birds are seen on average twice a week and at this point, cannot be considered rare, but instead uncommon.

KNOT BAD
Information on a Banded Red Knot

A walk along the beach near the opening to Tisbury Great Pond, near dusk on the 31st of July, was not only extraordinarily pleasant but produced an important and rare sighting of a color marked sandpiper. This observation of the red knot was very fortuitous.

Red knots are the second largest *Calidris* sandpiper, a large and diverse genus of birds. The largest member of this genus is the great knot that breeds in northern Siberia and winters in Australasia. Red knots (knots for the rest of this piece) are tremendous long-distance migrants. They congregate in large numbers at only a few specific localities at a specific time, so they are very susceptible to environmental or other disasters.

The world's authority on this species and author of *Flight of the Red Knot*, Brian Harrington, is based at the Manomet Center for Conservation Science (formerly the

Manomet Bird Observatory or MBO). He informed me that knots were only banded in the sequence and color pattern of my sighted knot in central coastal Argentina. An international group has been picking sites around the globe and attempting to capture, band, and color mark birds in the Austral summer or Northern Hemisphere winter where the birds spend a portion of their year.

The knot, one of a flock of seven individuals we could see on the beach along the middle south shore of Martha's Vineyard on 31 July 1998, was caught and banded with an orange band and a red band on its right leg, and an aluminum and a blue band on its left leg two winters ago in South America at Cabo San Antonio Oeste (southeast of Buenos Aires), a large sandy shallow estuarine environment perfect for knots.

After returning north and another nesting season it proceeded south, quite possibly stopping at the same spot on the Vineyard, before heading all the way back to Argentina to winter. Then it repeated the cycle and was spotted on its way south the next time, a year later by some very lucky observers with a good scope. There are very few banding returns or sightings of color coded birds that get reported to the researchers. Next time you're on the beach, take a close look at those sandpipers.

---

21 *August 1998*

The summer of '98 has been hot and humid, sultry, and uncomfortably sticky. On a global scale, July '98 was the hottest month ever and atmospheric scientists appear correct in their predictions about greenhouse gases and environmental changes wrought by humans. These conditions are what one expects to encounter in the southeast part of the country, but not here on the Vineyard with the cooling influence of the waters and afternoon sea breezes.

It is with a sigh of relief that as I write this I feel a cool, dry northwest wind just beginning to gently puff through my screen. There is a long narrow band of thunderstorms approaching, representing the border between two very different air masses. The thunderstorms are the real physical barrier between two sides of the frontal system: the hot and cold, the low and high pressure struggling for supremacy in the atmosphere.

This is the season that gives reason for a person interested in fish, birds, butterflies, the vagaries of light and sky conditions, and the phenomenom of migration to feel truly lucky to live in such a perfect geographical location. In late August, September, and October, the Vineyard becomes the funnel in the night sky that collects migrant birds and deposits them for the observers fortunate to live here, like an early holiday gift, fallen from the sky.

The waters south of the Vineyard have had very few birds on them compared with past years. Andy Goldman took his boat *Heritage* offshore approximately fifty miles on the 13th, accompanied by Matt Pelikan, Kienan Lacey, Jim Feiner, and this writer. There were a few scattered greater shearwaters, a manx shearwater, one Wilson's

storm petrel, and an adult pomarine jaeger seen. A lone
fin whale and a pod of common dolphins provided some
excitement but it was pretty quiet.

This past week has found lots of migrants islandwide.
The fields at Katama have had as many as six hundred
black-bellied plovers, eight hundred semipalmated
plovers, three American golden plovers, forty-five killdeer,
eighteen upland sandpipers, thirty-five bobolinks, four
whimbrels, and constantly hunting northern harriers and
red-tailed hawks. There are also hundreds of butterflies
and marauding dragonflies. Both cuckoo species, black-
billed and yellow-billed, have been widely reported and
warblers have begun to appear at the usual migrant traps.

Any grove of trees along the edges of fields or ponds
can attract migrant land birds. The trees are much more
attractive than the surrounding waters or open country,
which provide no food or cover for a migrant songbird.
Northern waterthrushes, yellow warblers, redstarts, and
red-eyed vireos have been on the move. Bobolinks are
heard calling overhead at night or seen in fields as they
have begun their remarkable journey south across the
Americas to winter in grasslands in northern Argentina.

26 *AUGUST* 1994
The autumn of '94 has already been memorable for the
fabulous numbers of shorebirds. And it is only the last
week of August with the meat of the migration still to
come. While the maximum number of high Arctic nesting

shorebirds has passed, peak diversity for both shorebird species and migrant landbirds is quickly approaching. Habitat for migrant plovers and sandpipers has never been better on the Vineyard.

The closure to vehicular traffic on Norton's Point has provided some unexpected dividends. Plant life both on the beach and along the tidal areas has been allowed to grow. The beach grass, of the genus *Ammophila*, has flourished and is quickly stabilizing an unstable area. And the presence of marsh grass more commonly known as cord grass, in the genus *Spartina*, sprouting all along the bay side is the beginning of a very productive tidal area beneficial to fisheries.

The nor'easter that began last Sunday night on the 21st and continued until late on the night of the 23rd forced many migrating shorebirds to pay the island an unexpected visit. In the teeth of the wind on Monday afternoon, the 22nd, near the entrance to Tisbury Great Pond a flock of forty-five greater yellowlegs attracted a few other species, including three Hudsonian godwits and a couple of whimbrels. The Hudsonian godwit is a very scarce species that breeds north and west of Hudson's Bay in Canada and winters in southern Argentina all the way to eastern Tierra del Fuego. It is rarely seen on the Vineyard.

Also on the 22nd on the flats at the mouth of Tisbury Great Pond was an amazing aggregation of "peeps." Peeps are commonly known as LBJ's, which stands for little brown jobs. There are five species of very similar small sandpipers and many birdwatchers have trouble telling them apart. Check out your favorite field guide for a look at these small but resilient sandpipers. There were approximately eight hundred of these birds, compromising four species, feeding vigorously on the flats. Most were semipalmated sandpipers with a few least sandpipers but amazingly, by actual count, there were sixty-eight white-rumped sandpipers and at least one western sandpiper. There has never been anything close to this number of white-rumps reported from the island before.

Richard Emmet of Vineyard Haven has been out and about and seen some very good birds. On the 17th in Chilmark he saw a buff-breasted sandpiper, an immature little blue heron, and a stilt sandpiper. This is very early for buff-breast and the only reported stilt sandpiper for '94 from the Vineyard. All three species are rare on the Vineyard. Flora Epstein of Chilmark spotted a blue-gray gnatcatcher at Roaring Brook on the 17th.

Black terns continue to be seen everywhere and in good numbers.

For fishermen, birders, and any outdoor enthusiast, the weather is endlessly fascinating. With the additions of weather channels on tv and radio, it is possible to follow the weather twenty-four hours a day. During the "swing season"—the transition of summer into fall—people of the Cape and surrounding islands become slightly obsessed with weather predictions. Hurricanes may arrive when most activities are at their best, especially fishing. The number of people, houses, and boats that needs to be tended to is overwhelming. Although winter northeast storms may be as powerful, last longer, and cause more coastal erosion, they are not nearly as feared or dangerous as hurricanes. Storm preparations are less formidable because summer visitors are gone, summer homes are snugly buttoned down, and most boats are safely stored on land. But when an Atlantic tropical storm is developing in August and September, people sit up and take notice. Anxious preparations to protect life and property get underway.

Both hurricanes and nor'easters generally approach our area from the south. All storms in the Northern Hemisphere rotate counterclockwise. The wind speeds on the right side of the storm, if you are facing the direction the storm is coming from, are increased by the storm's forward motion while the wind speeds of the left side are reduced by this same motion. This fantastically spinning right side of the storm is called the dangerous semicircle.

Winds in the right side of the storm blow from the southeast and southwest and the winds in the left side blow from the northeast and northwest. The speed and direction of the storm winds depend on the track of the eye of the storm. Storm paths to the west of the Cape and islands place us in the dangerous semicircle with the strongest winds. Storm paths that pass to the east produce winds with less velocity, which is easier on our region.

For vessels at sea, the large waves generated by the winds are extremely hazardous. Along the coast, extra-high storm tides may flood coastal lowlands. The ferocious winds cause killer waves containing tons of water, literally raising the sea level. As the winds drive the waves higher, the barometric pressure also drops, causing an additional rise in water level. These towering waves and higher sea levels are part of the storm surge, the most dangerous threat to the coast.

Funnel-shaped embayments like Buzzard's Bay increase the storm surge, which then floods the upper reaches of the bay. Additionally, storm rains can cause serious stream flooding, and the winds can topple trees and blow down buildings.

A fast-forming and quick-moving little hurricane named Bob hit the island on 19 August 1991. It formed a day or so earlier off the southeast coast of the United

States and made landfall just to the west of the Cape and islands. It developed so rapidly there was little warning. While it was designated a category 3 storm, in many places it was not as destructive to waterfront property as the 1938 and 1954 storms. Nonetheless, Hurricane Bob caused over a billion dollars in damage.

Thanks to Hurricane Bob, a new generation knows what a hurricane can do. But those who experienced Bob may be complacent and be caught unprepared by a larger storm. Some believe that the island will be safe for another decade or two, which is nonsense. Each year many tropical storms develop into hurricanes, and their paths are random. Thus, in any given year we could suffer the fate of that infamous 1954 hurricane season. New England was hit and trashed by Hurricane Carol in August, Hurricane Edna in September, and Hurricane Hazel in October!

From a birder's perspective, hurricanes are heaven. The bigger the storm, the more birds it may displace. After a hurricane has roared up the coast, the Vineyard can have the feel of a beach in Florida or the Carolinas. While no two hurricanes are the same, they all hold promise and once-in-a-lifetime opportunities for birders.

Pelagic birds ride on the outer bands of the powerful storms and get carried out of the tropics. Others get trapped in the calm eye and move north with it. While this is thrilling for the observer, it can be fatal for the individual birds, from sooty and bridled terns, tropicbirds, various shearwaters, and petrels to near-shore coastal species like royal terns, sandwich terns, and brown pelicans.

Storms occurring in late August, September, or October can transform a commonplace migration, bringing the exotic and the unexpected. But choose your poison, to wish for such an awesome display is to also place life and limb—human and animal, built and natural environments—at great risk.

Fall

"Days decrease,
    And autumn grows,
autumn is everything."
        —*Robert Browning*

THERE IS NO BETTER TIME or place than Martha's Vineyard in the fall—birding is as good as it gets. Migratory instincts are powerful and insatiable, and the night sky turns into an avian highway. The possibilities are truly without limit. Those of us lucky enough to live here have come to recognize this is as season without equal. To beachcombers, epicures, fishermen, gardeners, sightseers, and birders, this is no news flash.

September, October, and to a lesser degree, November are spectacular months. The absolute peak for maximum number of birds and species diversity generally occurs sometime in early October. Insectivorous birds head south for the winter along with everything else that migrates, from most bird families, to several bat species, to hordes of monarchs—the large orange and black butterflies that fly all the way to central Mexico—and several other species of butterflies, dragonflies, and many marine species, including bluefish, striped bass, bonito, etc.

And just when you think you have it figured out and know with some certainty when the birds are going to move, you can come up empty. The old adage of If at first you don't succeed, try, try, again really means go birding every morning in the fall. This way you will be on hand when the big flights occur. It can happen once a season or twice in one week. The only way to know is to be there.

It's addictive and frustrating. Everything is on the wing and confusing—which bird is which, how many, how few. It has been described as a narcotic; one enthusiastic birder portrays himself as in constant need of another fix.

Bird numbers are at an annual high with all the young birds, and like all rookies they make mistakes and stray from their normal range. You have to learn to expect the unexpected. Take a second look at all the common birds and make sure they are what they appear to be. You can't identify rare birds until you know the common ones.

Birders feel the same urge as the migrants and tend to flock at this time of year. The Vineyard is teaming with observers—good news since many more exciting events will be seen and reported. An area can be completely different from hour to hour, particularly an area like the Gay Head Cliffs. Arriving at dawn there can be hundreds, even thousands of birds overhead, and an hour later there may not be a bird in the sky. By midmorning a flight of diurnal migrating hawks may be streaming along the cliffs. Each group of birders at the same place at different times of the day will see completely different birds.

September

SEPTEMBER HAS FINALLY ARRIVED. For birders this is the equivalent of meeting the president, winning the Super Bowl and the seventh game of the NBA finals, and hitting the lottery for the biggest jackpot ever, all at the same time.

Shorebirds, seabirds, land birds, warblers, vireos, and flycatchers are at a zenith. This is prime time—the ornithological equivalent of February sweeps.

September is magnificent. Even when a stagnant weather pattern hangs on for a few days, there are still more birds here both in terms of numbers of species and individuals than at any other time of year.

Unlike a passenger in modern jet aircraft, the bird actually propels itself as well as navigates, avoids speedy predators in the air and stealthy mammals on the ground, eats, drinks, bathes, and carries on all bodily functions as it migrates south.

Habitat loss along coastal areas that birds depend upon as staging and feeding areas is a threat to birds in migration. Birds are severely affected as subdivisions and condominiums replace the thickets formerly full of berries and bugs. They are running out of places to rest, which makes natural environments increasingly rare and important.

The month of September seems to pass in a flash. While the calendar maintains there are thirty days, it feels more like a very short week.

―――――

4 SEPTEMBER 1998

The first of the month arrived this past Monday, breaking out of the stagnant weather patterns of the recent past. The weather was extraordinary, clear blue skies, dry air, unlimited visibility, and a nice midseventies temperature. Finally gone was the tropical humidity and heat that plagued us most of the summer.

Birding is most popular around the warm days near summer's end. Most impressive and unusual for the Vineyard were the sightings of Hudsonian godwits. The morning of the 27th after a noisy and wet evening of thunderstorms, this writer and his son were fortunate to be on Norton's Point at first light. We were treated to views of lots of grounded shorebirds, with white-rumped sandpipers, American oystercatchers, lesser yellowlegs, and short-billed dowitchers along the shore. There were two flocks of Hudsonian godwits that were grounded from the night's storms. We watched as a group departed straight south over the ocean, climbing into the still overcast and foggy sky, calling softly to each other, giving contact notes designed to keep them together. All the godwits were adult birds molting from breeding to winter plumage.

12 SEPTEMBER 1997

The weather has been mired in a stagnant stretch of mediocrity. While powerful Hurricane Erica rumbles around south and east of Bermuda, a weak frontal system has stalled over the island, maintaining bland weather. Yet it is prime time, and even with the absence of any significant weather systems, there have been lots of birds around.

One long-distance migrant that is a rare visitor, almost annual, is the buff-breasted sandpiper. These oddly shaped sandpipers have big bodies, long skinny necks, and little heads. They have very long wings and use them to make an elliptical annual migration from above the Arctic Circle to the pampas of Argentina. In spring, they go up the middle of the United States, but in the fall some move singly or in small numbers down the East Coast.

A buff-breasted sandpiper was discovered on the southeast corner of Chappaquiddick on the 7th by Mary Mira, Charlie and Mebbit Morano, Bob Larsen, Barbara Rubin, Lin Fagan, and this writer. The bird was an adult with a uniformly buffy, pumpkin color that extended from the bill all the way to the undertail coverts. This is the first one that any of the group had ever seen in this plumage on the Vineyard. Normally, we see immature birds with a buffy breast, perhaps with a little bit of color extending down onto the belly but then fading to gray or white. The bird was very tame. The worn feathers on the mantle and scapulars, frayed at the edges, were interesting to see.

While watching the buff-breasted sandpiper on the

9th, we saw a parasitic jaeger leisurely heading east right down the beach. Its falconlike demeanor sent all the shorebirds into the air as they recognized this raptorial predator in gull-like garb. A couple of days earlier, the group watched an immature female Cooper's hawk launch a clumsy attack, twice, over the pond at the shorebirds and ducks, which all easily eluded the inexperienced strafe.

Just down the beach, perched on a snow fence, was a female yellow-headed blackbird. This most distinctive blackbird is subtle when viewed from the back but when it turns, it is unmistakable. It is a midwestern and western species that occasionally wanders to the East Coast in the fall. This is the first one on the island in several years. The bird was obviously tired and repeatedly closed its eyes as it allowed views from eight to ten feet away, seemingly unconcerned. It hopped on the sand between the beach grass looking for seeds.

An American pipit was spotted flying along the flats at Norton's Point on the 8th by Matt Pelikan. This is several weeks earlier than these birds usually appear. The Gay Head Cliffs have been a little slow but still there have been good numbers of bobolinks, cedar waxwings, small numbers of orioles, brown-headed cowbirds, house finches, and robins. Red-breasted nuthatches are starting out on an irruptive pattern and have been moving everywhere.

Another species apparently poised to irrupt this year is the white-winged crossbill. This spruce-loving finch has not been seen on the island in any kind of flight year in over a dozen years. They have suddenly begun showing up the last couple of days all over eastern Massachusetts and after the next northwest wind should appear over Vineyard shores. Hawks have started to move and a smattering of sharp-shinned, Cooper's, and northern harriers are seen almost daily. Falcons are starting their push south with merlins leading the charge.

A couple of nighthawks were reported this past week. This abundant caprimulgid is common inland and flights of hundreds, even thousands are recorded along the Connecticut and Housatonic Rivers in central and western Massachusetts. They are always a good find on the island.

20 SEPTEMBER 1996

While September is always great birding, this past week was way above expectations, indeed off the charts. The birding was, in a word, awesome. Where to begin? Start at the beginning and go as far as you can sounds right, so here goes.

The weather has been less than ideal for outside activities and rain, fog, and general dreariness have been the norm. This has severely impeded bird migration and made it difficult for land birds to move south. The passing of yet another hurricane to the east has been detrimental to migrating shorebirds.

Whenever there has been any kind of clear night with light north or westerly winds, birds have been on the move. The night of the 10th was one such evening and dawn brought partially overcast conditions with a wind that soon turned northeast. Nonetheless, there were impressive numbers of migrant birds departing the Vineyard from the Gay Head Cliffs.

Jeff Verner and this writer were there and observed over one thousand warblers, unidentified as to species, flying overhead calling, heading back to the mainland. The birds were in small groups occasionally numbering as many as twenty-five birds in a loose mixed flock. Hundreds of bobolinks, cedar waxwings, and red-winged blackbirds were going off. A small flight of three kestrels, a dickcissel, and an American golden plover were all right at the circle. A Lincoln's sparrow in the thicket near the lighthouse was the season's first.

The best bird of the day and one that is rare, especially in this plumage in the fall, was seen just before lunch in Vineyard Haven by Gus Daniels. Working in his greenhouse watering orchids, he glanced out in the yard and was shocked to see a brilliant male hooded warbler flitting outside his window. This bright yellow warbler with black hood and white tail spots is one of the gems of the bird world. It was the 150th species of bird that Gus has seen in or from his yard.

Hurricane Hortense luckily—it being Friday the 13th—roared by several hundred miles east of the Vineyard but still brought heavy rains, strong northeasterly winds, and spectacular surf that had the island's intrepid surfers out in force.

The flight of American golden plovers was historic. Such numbers of these birds had not been seen on the

Vineyard in well over a century. Flocks of anywhere from twenty to forty-five individual birds would appear high in the sky calling from a northeasterly direction. The American golden plovers on the ground would answer and the airborne birds would drop down a little for a closer look, before proceeding south/southwest flying very fast with a thirty-knot tailwind. Their ground speed must have been close to a hundred miles an hour.

There were at least 256 American golden plovers seen by actual count with the bulk continuing south. There were flocks scattered around the fields and there were groups of twenty-five and thirty as well as smaller groups all around the fields. Over two hundred birds were observed arriving from the northeast and just doing a flyby. During the morning hours the American golden plovers outnumbered the black-bellied plovers.

The wet fields offered food and shelter to all kinds of shorebirds and gulls. The fields, full of earthworms, acted like a magnet for the birds. Among the mixed flocks of shorebirds were seventy lesser yellowlegs, fifty pectoral sandpipers, a stilt sandpiper (the only one seen on the island this year), three white-rumped sandpipers, several dowitchers, ninety semipalmated plovers, and a smattering of other shorebirds.

The cliffs at Gay Head were fantastic in the early morning hours. Highlights included all three species of local falcons: merlins, kestrels, and a peregrine falcon that "ringed" (a falconer's term) and then stooped on a group of hapless warblers. The falcon hit a doomed warbler, then rolled over and caught it, administering a death blow with its beak. It then began to pluck the bird on the wing and continued heading towards Block Island.

Other hawk highlights included Cooper's hawks, sharp-shinned, and ospreys. Land bird highlights were blue grosbeaks, purple martins, a lark sparrow, a dickcissel, blue-gray gnatcatchers, a warbling vireo, yellow-breasted chat, Nashville, prairie, magnolia, blackpoll, and several other species of warbler.

23 SEPTEMBER 1994

The weather, the birds, it's too much for one's senses. Only one week left in this glorious month. Birds from tiny hummingbirds to large gannets, geese, and swans are migrating around, over, and on Martha's Vineyard. The skies, seas, and swamps are full of life in September.

Falcons top off this incredible month. Kestrels, the smallest of North American falcons, have been widespead with several groups of four or five birds being seen. Peregrine falcons are the world's most widespread falcon species, ranging throughout the globe, and the fastest of flying birds at up to two hundred miles per hour in dive-bombing, or stooping flight. One individual was seen digesting a meal off the cliffs on No Man's Land last Sunday the 18th and another was seen "on point," if you will, high above Wasque effortlessly hanging and watching for a suitable target. Numbers of these birds are migrating by now and numbers increase until about the 10th of October.

The bird reports are fast and furious this time of year

and almost every day some interesting, unusual, or rare
birds are spotted.

The Magician

The Vineyard has an annual phenomenon that coincides
nicely with the Martha's Vineyard Striped Bass and Bluefish
Derby. While the fishing is excellent and fishermen are out in
force, the annual southbound passage of one of the most exciting birds in the world, a small falcon called the merlin, is
taking place. Merlins are slightly smaller than pigeons, but
are built for speed and are extraordinary to watch in the air.

All falcons have long pointed wings, long tails, vision that
is eight to ten times better than a human's, long pointed
talons that act as midair grappling hooks, and tremendous
powers of flight. They specialize in capturing other birds in
the air. Because of their superior speed, they prefer open
country and love coastlines and offshore islands. The Vineyard is one of the best places in the world to see merlins.

Merlins are the ultimate hawks. Because of their relatively
small size, they generally capture small birds and eat two
daily, on average. Unlike a red-tailed hawk that will circle
broadly, or an osprey that flaps along occasionally hovering,
the merlin is a speeding bullet that demands control of all
the airspace.

Merlins are feisty and arrogant, attacking and dive-bombing any other bird that is in the air. They can't seem to help
themselves as they dive on and harass eagles, red-tails,

goshawks, and even peregrine falcons. They may look like mosquitoes next to eagles, but merlins just have to take a run at the big birds. They have no concept of fear.

Merlins breed across the top of the Northern Hemisphere in the spruce belt. They are much more common in North America than in Europe or northern Asia. A few pairs have recently been found nesting in New York's Adirondack Mountains and at least a few pairs are breeding in the north woods of Maine. They breed in New Brunswick and sparingly in Nova Scotia, becoming more common closer to the taiga. They are the most common nesting bird of prey in Iceland. It is late September and the peak numbers of this species are passing by. Pay attention, you will see them.

Merlins and peregrine falcons regularly travel long distances over open water. They routinely cross the Gulf of Maine and the Gulf of Mexico on migration and three or four hundred miles of open water is absolutely no problem for them. During migration, the ocean is a large floating snack bar for these talented speedsters.

The next time you're on the beach and you're lucky enough to see a streaking blur it is undoubtedly a merlin chasing its anticipated next meal. It's showtime so keep your eyes to the sky and watch for merlin, the magician.

OCTOBER

"O suns and skies and clouds of June / And flowers of June together / Ye cannot rival for one hour / October's bright blue weather." —*Helen Hunt Jackson*

SAY HELLO TO OCTOBER and all it has to offer. October is a little cooler than September, and even better for large numbers of common and unusual birds.

Not to mention that there are even fewer people and fewer parking hassles!

The birding community awaits this season giddily. One of the most striking sights of October is the movement of hawks. Days with strong northwesterly winds are sure to bring some hawks and migratory raptors.

The peak of the falcon and accipiter migration occurs sometime in early to midmonth and they are joined by a respectable number of other diurnal migrating raptors. The island has far and away the best flight of peregrine falcons and accipiters in Massachusetts. The outer beaches on Chappaquiddick, the entire south shore of the island, Squibnocket, and Gay Head are the places that always seem to feature the most birds.

A day afield virtually assures one a look at the powerful

and fast peregrine falcon. Whenever the wind is from a westerly direction, the cliffs at Gay Head are sure to play host to as many as eight different peregrines, all hanging in the air at the same time. The first three weeks of October are the best time.

Recently forty-two individual peregrines came by the cliffs and headed straight out over the water towards Block Island over the course of two-and-a-half hours mid-morning. The birds were spectacular as they "appeared" over the cliff hanging like winged scimitars, waiting and watching for an opportunity to catch a meal.

The stronger the wind velocity, the more fun it is to watch these masters of the air. By adjusting the pitch and sweep of their wings, they are able to hang motionless, then swoop down, diving like missiles, then instantly pop back up to their original position. All this without having to flap or use any energy. Their silhouettes strike terror in the bird world.

Most of the peregrines that migrate past Vineyard shores are breeders in the high Arctic and Greenland. The race that breeds in Greenland is large and the immature bird possesses a blonde head and brown back. Both adult and young birds frequent the cliffs and the entire shoreline of the Vineyard in the fall. The immatures often practice their flying skills at the expense of great black-backed gulls, herring gulls, and cormorants who learn quickly to get out of the way even if it means diving underwater in full flight.

This is also the time of the big sparrow flights. Some mornings after the passage of a cold front, there are thousands of migrant birds all over the island on road edges and in fields. Some mornings they seem to be everywhere as they search for a suitable feeding area. White-crowned and white-throated sparrows, swamp, chipping, savannah, and juncos can all be seen some mornings. Add late departing warblers, vireos, other primarily insectivorous birds, and large numbers of frugivores, including cedar waxwings and robins, and you have only scratched the surface of October's offerings.

Waterfowl begin moving in earnest as long flocks (tens of thousands) of sea ducks and skeins of geese begin appearing overhead and along the shores. Smaller numbers of arriving overwinterers like buffleheads, goldeneyes, and mergansers add to the profusion. Often hundreds of common and red-throated loons are winging overhead or cruising offshore with their distinctive manner of flight and their unique silhouettes. Horned and red-necked grebes appear in saltwater, pied-billed grebes in fresh. Birds abound in island ponds and estuaries.

Great blue herons are migrating south in considerable numbers, as large as bald eagles on the wing. Loose flocks of ten to thirty often pass by high overhead. When the sun reflects off the head of an individual bird and makes it appear white, the bird looks much like an eagle. Seeing them as a flock eliminates that possibility, although innumerable times in the past thirty years I've rushed off a

major highway to investigate the sight of a large solitary
bird. Most of the time it turns out to be a great blue, but
occasionally, just occasionally, it is an eagle soaring and
heading south. It is always worth checking.

———

6 OCTOBER 1996

Land's end is the place to be when hunting for unusual
migrant species. And just that has happened with the
discovery of a bird on 30 September at Katama Farm in
Edgartown. A northern wheatear was found at 4 PM by
infrequent island visitors Chris and Norma Floyd of
Lexington, MA.

Northern wheatears are remarkable little birds that per-
form an annual migration that is, without a doubt, the
longest journey undertaken by any land bird on the planet.
There are many species of wheatears in Asia and Africa
but we are concerned with the northern wheatear (*Oenanthe oenanthe*). All wheatears winter in Africa with a few
remaining along the northern Mediterranean Sea. They
nest across most of the top of the Northern Hemisphere.

In spring they head north along two very different
routes. One part of the population moves north through
Europe, with some staying to breed in Scandinavia.
Others cross to Iceland, then to Greenland, then across
to Baffin Island and Labrador in the eastern Canadian
Arctic. They nest along this entire route and each year
colonize further west. Beginning in August, they retrace

their route to Africa. Another part of the population leaves Africa and heads northeast, to Asia and Siberia, while others cross the Bering Strait to breed across Alaska and the Yukon. Each year they expand further east. In fall they follow the same route back to Africa, via the Middle East.

Wheatear sightings have risen dramatically in the last five years. In fact, after a lack of sightings for over thirty years on the Vineyard, wheatears have been seen in September for three years consecutively. One possibility is that a small number of birds is already wintering somewhere in the Americas, perhaps in Patagonia.

13 OCTOBER 1995

Monday the 9th, Columbus Day, broke clear and cool with a light northwesterly wind that faded to calm by afternoon. Following the delayed frontal systems that kept the weather wet, cool, and cloudy for the preceding several days, it was like opening the flood gates. Sunrise on the Gay Head Cliffs was outrageous and so were the numbers of birds. Several observers likened it to the Hitchcock movie. Birds were everywhere from 7 AM until about 10:30 AM. One of the largest flights of sharp-shinned hawks ever recorded in Massachusetts was seen, and there were hordes of migrant land birds.

Juncos and sparrows were all over in great numbers. Attempting to estimate numbers of individuals was difficult, but juncos numbered in groups of hundreds and approximately two thousand birds were within a mile of

the cliffs. Both ruby-crowned and golden-crowned
kinglets had a big nocturnal movement and these minute
olive birds were numbering in the hundreds. White-
throated, white-crowned, swamp, savannah, field, and
chipping sparrows were also widespread.

The cliffs and surrounding areas were teeming with
avian life all heading to the west. Woodpeckers—flickers,
downy, hairy, red-bellied, and the infamous yellow-bellied
sapsucker—were all seen flying around the cliffs. Cat-
birds, mockingbirds, and brown thrashers were in small
flocks. The place was rocking and no two observers were
looking at the same birds.

17 OCTOBER 1997

A better stretch of weather is hard to recall, every day
another perfect bull's-eye. Even if there were no birds flying, rising early and witnessing the spectacular sunrises
on a dead calm morning would be enough. The wind,
remarkably, has stayed down and uncharacteristically
remained light and variable for days on end. While this
slows down the visible hawk migration, it is ideal for small
song birds that fly all night long.

Large numbers of birds have been moving and the
morning of Columbus Day, the 12th, found impressive
numbers of birds departing Martha's Vineyard for points
south and west. Just before sunrise on the cliffs at Gay
Head, little chips, ticks, whistles, thin little trills, and other
migrant bird call notes were coming out of the sky from all

directions. Some of these calls were recognizable as
robins, cedar waxwings, American pipits, purple finches,
yellow-rumped and palm warblers, red-winged and rusty
blackbirds, common grackles, brown-headed cowbirds,
eastern meadowlarks, eastern bluebirds, dark-eyed juncos, and a myriad of other birds.

With the conditions remaining so still, bird call notes
were able to be detected at a much greater distance than
usual. Most of this month has been as quiet as a sound stu-
dio and audio conditions have never been as good. The
drawback of having little or no wind is that the migrating
birds fly higher. So while one can often hear them, you can
not locate them visually overhead.

There have been many ornithological highlights this
past week. Virtually all bird species have been migrating,
but the bulk of the insectivorous birds are past, and large
numbers of loons, gannets, waterfowl, frugivores, and
sparrows are the main event at this stage of October.

On the 8th, Lanny McDowell saw a bird that has not
been seen in approximately eighteen years on the island:
a Henslow's sparrow, a small, big-headed, short-tailed
species with an olive colored head and some fine streaking on the breast.

A highlight from the 12th was an attack by a peregrine
falcon on a migrating shorebird. The falcon was spotted as
it came off the cliffs, flying powerfully in a full climb. The
bird was ringing, climbing in a circular fashion, intent on
the prey, cutting it off from the ground. The falcon kept

climbing with incredibly fast wing beats, almost out of sight of binoculars. Finally the target came into view: a long-billed shorebird, either a snipe or a woodcock.

The shorebird folded up and dove for cover and the falcon followed suit in an awesome stoop. The woodcock was dropping like shot out of a cannon, but the falcon was a blur and gaining rapidly. Nearing the ground at break-neck speed, the falcon about to strike the woodcock, the shorebird made a little twist towards some telephone wires as the duo appeared about to collide with the ground. The falcon went roaring by just missing the woodcock. Instead of diving into the thicket, the woodcock began climbing out over the water, with the now tired hawk in pursuit. Eventually the woodcock climbed up and away, and the falcon gave up. Whew! Enough for now.

21 OCTOBER 1998

Spectacular wrong-way storm-assisted migration dumped birds on the Vineyard. An unusual weather pattern that ruined many outdoor Columbus Day weekend activities in the northeastern United States delivered an astonishing variety and number of birds to very specific areas of the northeast and southern Nova Scotia. The fast-moving low pressure system raced up along and off the coast, finally depositing its airborne cargo over the weekend. Unprecedented and heretofore unknown numbers of warblers, vireos, tanagers, grosbeaks, and buntings were displaced by this odd fall storm.

In the long ornithological history of the region, numbers like these had never happened, especially in mid-October. The event was similar in nature to fallouts following hurricanes, but these birds were not emaciated or beaten up, but healthy active birds.

The phenomenon of large numbers of storm-assisted (i.e. caused) displaced birds is well-known. The weather system that transported these birds was just like the northeast low pressure systems that occur in the spring, often grounding significant numbers of birds along the eastern seaboard. But this rarely happens in the fall. The species involved are mostly birds of the deep south that winter in eastern Mexico and Central America, not species commonly associated with routine overwater flights on the way to wintering grounds in the Caribbean.

The probable scenario is that the birds got airborne at dusk somewhere between Atlanta and New Orleans, and once aloft encountered the very strong and fast-moving low pressure system. They migrate, especially over open water, at high altitudes. The birds sensed and then encountered the approaching low pressure, accompanied by large amounts of precipitation, and turned to avoid the oncoming storm.

At night, with no stars visible because of persistent cloud cover, wanting to avoid the worst of the rain and fog, the birds flew out in front of the storm. They tried to stay out of and above the heavy rain and strongest winds. The storm traveled, with its avian complement, up out over the western North Atlantic skimming New England and southern Nova Scotia.

While humans were bemoaning the nasty weather, birds were beginning to appear in droves. It was as though someone flipped a switch to start the flow of unusual birds and then increased the power.

As reported in last week's column, there had been at least nine separate blue grosbeaks seen over the long holiday weekend on Martha's Vineyard. In a normal fall, an active observer might expect to see one or two individuals of this species, if lucky. This was just the tip of the iceberg, so to speak. On the 14th, sixteen individuals were seen, eclipsing the previous high count of fourteen individuals for the entire state that occurred on Nantucket in early October 1980.

The birds kept on coming. One can safely assume that only a fraction of actual birds here were seen and to think that over a hundred blue grosbeaks were on this island alone boggles the mind.

On the morning of the 14th a male prothonotary warbler was discovered dead alongside a parked car on Chappaquiddick. This southern species is always rare on the island and the fact that it was an adult male indicates it was caught up in the same weather system. On the 17th, a Le Conte's sparrow—a new species for the island—was found in some overgrown fields in West Tisbury. This secretive species had been seen fourteen times previously in Massachusetts, but never on Martha's Vineyard. Coupled with the Townsend's warbler, another new species for the island seen a couple of weeks ago, the Vineyard avifauna list is rapidly growing.

It will be interesting to see if there was an influx of North American birds to Iceland, Ireland, and the UK as a result of this truly no-name storm that transported so many birds the wrong way. The heavily birded Scilly Isles, off southwestern England, literally crawling with birding aficionados, should tell this story down the road.

25 OCTOBER 1996

Another week, another example of remarkable weather. Record amounts of rainfall, strong northeast winds, and extreme high tides combined with heavy surf caused beach erosion. But temperatures were fairly warm and the birding was terrific.

The big news was the discovery and identification of a species never before recorded for the island and a rare bird in this part of the world. The finding of this small, rather nondescript first winter gull was cause for considerable excitement in the birding community. The bird was a common gull, or mew gull (*Larus canus*), and it was found on Sunday morning, 20 October, feeding in the fields at Katama along with hundreds of more usual herring and ring-billed gulls.

The weather was horrible for observing the bird, but at the same time, without the rain, wind, and generally unpleasant conditions the bird would not have been there. Walking along in the field right next to this bird and the reason for its discovery were not one but two first-winter lesser black-backed gulls. At one point the three birds were all feeding within twenty feet of each other and were all bunched together in the binocular field of view. This was an exceptionally rare sight in North America and is something one might expect to find in Iceland, Ireland, or the UK, but not on Martha's Vineyard.

While out attempting to photograph the gull in the fields the next day, I saw a long-billed dowitcher in the field. This shorebird is extremely rare on the island and this is the first one found here in many years. The morning of the 20th also yielded two Leach's storm petrels in Sengekontacket Pond. These pelagic birds are rarely seen from shore except after strong northeasterly storms.

27 OCTOBER 1995

It's a rare October that brings us a good flight of snow geese. These white geese with black wing tips are generally smaller than the resident Canada geese and are heading south from breeding areas in the high Canadian, Alaskan, and northeastern Siberian Arctic. These birds are heading for wintering areas along the Chesapeake Bay and are so precise in navigating that they rarely get caught off course. Hearing and seeing a high-flying flock of wild geese migrating in the fall stirs some inner, ancient chord in the human brain.

Fishermen are known to tell fish stories, but it is not often that fishermen tell bird stories. This is a tale of a fishing trip off Wasque on Friday the 13th, the last day of the 1995 Martha's Vineyard Fishing Derby. Ned Casey and Tom Barlowski were out trying to catch a last-minute derby winner a couple of miles from the beach, when mid-morning they saw gulls chasing what they thought was a butterfly not far from the boat. Fascinated, they watched as the gulls twisted and turned in hot pursuit of what the men now realized was a very tired and scared small bird.

The gulls were relentless in their chase of the perceived easy meal. Ned and Tom watched and saw the exhausted bird knocked into the water. Not enjoying this scene, Ned turned the boat around and sped over to the bird before any of the gulls had gotten hold of it. He netted the catch and held in his hand a strikingly beautiful bird with a bright yellow breast, green back, and white spectacles around the eyes. He put it in a spot on the deck and forgot about it the rest of the day. The fishermen saw at least two other birds get caught and eaten by gulls as they attempted to approach the shore.

Their fishing over, they were almost into Tashmoo, when the bird, undoubtedly a yellow-breasted chat from the description, woke up, hopped about, and then flew ashore. That's no fish story!

November

"What is the late November doing, / With the disturbance of the spring." —*T.S. Eliot*

IN NOVEMBER WE SHIFT from daylight savings to eastern standard time, with constantly decreasing daylight and droves of arriving wintering bird life. Flocks of sea ducks move along all shorelines regardless of the time of day and numbers of land birds continue to go south.

The weather in November is characterized by strong, fast-moving frontal systems interspersed with lovely periods of Indian summer. The weather ranges from coastal storms with winds exceeding hurricane force to calm and sunny weather only twelve hours later. It is a month of extreme weather systems and a time of movement and turmoil for late migrating or lost birds.

November is the time for a classic nor'easter. Nor'easters are fearsome storms that generally last three days with gale-force winds, huge surf conditions, and lots of precipitation. These storms often drive pelagic species inshore and rarely big "wrecks" of alcids occur. Shearwaters, fulmars, and petrels (tubenoses) may be concentrated along shorelines or points. Dovekies are infamous for getting blown inland and along the beaches.

The Outer Cape is the best spot to see birds after a nor'easter. Cape Cod Bay is created by the long sweep of Cape Cod, which juts out east and then north into the North Atlantic Ocean. During a prolonged nor'easter oceanic birds get forced along the coast from Maine to Massachusetts. Heading south they follow the shore of Plymouth, Massachusetts. Here they are gradually turned east along the north shore of Cape Cod, then north as the Cape turns in Brewster, Orleans, and Eastham ending at Race Point in Provincetown.

When the birds reach the tip of the Cape they are once again forced into the teeth of the gale. After battling it for days, most turn and run with the wind back across the bay until they hit the shoreline on the south shore and repeat the loop around the north side of the Cape again. The longer the storm lasts, the more birds amass in this oblong circulation. The storm usually ends overnight with the arrival of a high-pressure cold front from Canada. First light brings improved visibility and a change in wind direction, so the birds make a mass exodus from Cape Cod Bay.

The stronger the front, the better the conditions are at First Encounter Beach in Eastham, which has a long parking lot in front of the salt marsh beach (where the Pilgrims first encountered Native Americans). The westerly winds force the birds along the bay shore of Eastham and Wellfleet and some truly staggering flights have occurred. After a huge nor'easter in early December a few years ago, an astounding twelve hundred jaegers, (falconlike seabirds) were seen, more than anyone had ever reported. It is one of the few places to see pelagic species without an obligatory boat trip.

The Vineyard can only compete with these opportunities on the Cape occasionally, after hurricanes or nor'easters. Then you might be able to see northern gannets, both red-necked and red phalaropes, pomarine and parasitic jaegers, fulmars, alcids including dovekies, razorbills, murres, and black-legged kittiwakes.

The island also offers abundant food for waterfowl, including sea ducks that congregate inshore.

The Vineyard is blessed with a remarkable number of wintering birds that live on the open ocean, tidal estuaries, and brackish ponds. Indeed, the number of sea ducks and, at times, loons can be staggering. Any morning at dawn out along East Beach on Chappaquiddick from now until March will reveal tens of thousands of sea ducks moving from nighttime resting areas to feeding grounds.

Enormous flocks of all three species of scoters, oldsquaws, and common eiders abound from Wasque to Gay Head. Martha's Vineyard may be the finest locale to see these northern sea ducks anywhere in North America, including common and red-throated loons, horned and red-necked grebes, northern gannets, and pelagics.

Every morning at dawn there is a tremendous amount of activity along the shorelines, especially on the south side of the island. Almost every kind of bird that spends its days on the water spends its nights resting on it. The nocturnal currents, waves, and winds move the birds

around. At first light they may have drifted miles from
their positions when "the lights went out." The birds
quickly lift off and realign themselves. Many species feed
in one area in the daytime and fly up to forty miles away to
overnight on the water elsewhere.

One of the most spectacular of these commutes is the
oldsquaws shuttling between their bedroom community
in Nantucket Sound to their watering holes of Nantucket
Shoals and south of the Vineyard. This passage takes
them past Nantucket, Tuckernuck, Muskeget, and Chappaquiddick Islands both at dawn and dusk.

The mass of ducks feed primarily on blue mussels,
which are in ample supply in shallow water between here
and Nantucket and along the south shore, especially up-
island. You can't miss these ducks, given their large size
and their distinctive patterns.

Snow buntings—remarkable small black, white, and
rust colored finches that breed the farthest north of any
land bird—generally appear in late October and early
November. November is also the time when wintering
birds are arriving, and if there are going to be any irrup-
tions of winter finches, shrikes, hawks, or owls, they begin
to manifest themselves by midmonth.

---

17 NOVEMBER 1995

The gales of November have been battering the island
with scarcely a lull in between. Nasty, windy, wet conditions with very strong winds have been the norm this past

week. Torrential wind-driven rain, occasional snow flurries, and roaring seas along the south shore have made islanders feel close to nature.

Over the top of the raging surf with breakers extending out to the horizon can be seen skeins of birds. They are moving to and fro, wheeling and turning above the maelstrom that is the surface of the ocean. Attempting to find a favorite mussel bed or some lee from the storm requires more energy with decreasing results. Even loons, grebes, and sea ducks tire of the high winds and restless seas as it becomes hard, if not impossible, to find food in the churning, murky water, let alone to sleep on the surface. Many birds are forced to relocate to calmer, less productive waters to ride out the storm.

Daily caloric needs are not met and fat reserves that will be needed later on, especially in a cold, icy winter, are tapped to weather the storm. Rough weather is hard on wintering marine bird populations, already gearing up for colder temperatures and decreasing supplies of both fin and shellfish.

It appears that northern shrikes and evening grosbeaks are going to be big this winter. Evening grosbeaks are one of the most beautiful finches in North America. They are widespread on the continent but irruptive in this part of the country. There have been virtually no grosbeaks on the Cape and islands for the past six years. All of a sudden there are reports of hundreds of these birds appearing in New England and the first two reported from the Vineyard showed up at Connie Cowan's bird feeder at Katama

on the 8th. More are expected. Northern shrikes, land
birds with perching feet but beaks like hawks, have been
widely reported the last week in Massachusetts, but none
has been spotted on the Vineyard yet.

20 NOVEMBER 1998

The season is rapidly changing from fall to winter. The
deciduous woodlands are stripped bare by wind and rain,
a few brown scraggly leaves tenuously holding on. The
beach grass and marsh grasses are silvery in winter garb,
and the days continue to shorten. Resting birds stand on
one leg, the other tucked into warm and insulating feathers, an energy conservation measure that reduces heat loss
by approximately half.

The ocean and sounds around the island take on a
very different look in November with the low angle of the
sun reflecting off the gun-metal gray surface. Far from
inviting, the waters look ominous.

The first fall storm of the season hit on the 11th with
sustained wind and rain from the southeast and south for
only about a half day. It was enough to force earthworms
from the soggy fields at Katama and for the opportunistic
gulls to find them. Approximately one thousand gulls
descended on the fields in the late afternoon and put on a
terrific display.

Amongst the abundant (900 plus) herring gulls and
100 ring-billed gulls were several other rarely encountered
species. A first-winter glaucous gull, a large white-winged
gull with a light pink bill with black tip, was enjoying

the feast. Another white-winged gull, an Iceland gull, was also nearby. It was diminutive compared to the larger glaucous and its tiny solid black bill and comparatively longer wings made for an excellent lesson in how to separate these two species.

Scattered among the throng were three lesser black-backed gulls, recent and increasing émigrés from Europe. An adult, a second winter, and a first-winter bird were all resting and/or chowing earthworms among their congeners. They are becoming a regular occurrence in our area and almost routine in fields after big winds and rain. A lone Bonaparte's gull and several laughing gulls were also in the crowd. Four snow geese dropped in.

The flats and fields at Katama have been hosting a surprising number of lingering shorebirds. These birds were still present on the 18th and had been there all week. Some birds move back and forth from the flats to the fields. There was a large flock of black-bellied plovers reaching a high of 800 birds on the 14th. American pipits have been all over and very tame, which is not usual behavior for these hard-to-see small birds that breed in the Arctic tundra.

Over on the flats on the 14th was a first-winter common tern. These birds departed our area very early this year and this one is around more than two months after the other members of its species went south. Occasional peregrine falcons and merlins sporadically hunt this area. The more common northern harrier, which is a rodent specialist that hunts exclusively in open beach, marsh, and grassland habitats, is frequently encountered.

Last, a relatively rare bird appeared in a very unusual place not far from downtown on the 16th. Willy DeBettencourt, a ridiculously hard-working mechanic and fixer of anything with engines, noted a small dark bird bobbing around on top of a small pile of tires outside of Bink's Auto Repair in Oak Bluffs. Fortuitously, this writer happened to wander by at the same time and was amazed to find a diminutive winter wren standing like some proud miniature rooster. This scarce wren is never common on the island and usually is found skulking around like a mouse in stone walls up-island. The bird then flew off and disappeared into some garbage cans. The world's most streetwise wren.

25 NOVEMBER 1994

Birds were very popular yesterday, Thanksgiving, aka turkey day. This traditional American holiday gets more of our population moving than any other. It's like a mass migration of very short duration. An estimated 98 percent of the population ate the bird, yesterday, that Ben Franklin nominated to be the national bird instead of the scavenging, carrion- and offal-eating bald eagle. Most turkeys that were consumed by modern day Pilgrims were not wild birds and were raised expressly for holiday feasts. Wild turkeys were extirpated as breeding birds in Massachusetts about 1850, due to extreme hunting pressure and the lack of any game laws.

Efforts to reestablish this formerly abundant native

species began in the 1920s. Turkeys were introduced at
Naushon Island in 1929, 1938, 1939, and 1940, and in the
Myles Standish State Forest, Plymouth (landing site of
the *Mayflower*) in 1966. These efforts were not successful
and birds were last seen on Naushon in 1976. Turkeys
were introduced in the Quabbin area during the 1950s,
and as many as twenty-five to forty birds have been seen
there in groups through the 1980s. Most birds seen in the
last twenty years are derived from Pennsylvania stocks
released in Berkshire County, where the species is now
well established. The status on the Vineyard is confusing,
but turkeys can be encountered almost anywhere at any
time. Whether these are "wild" birds remains a question,
most are quite tame and can be easily approached. Elsewhere in Massachusetts, wild turkeys are sufficiently
established that an open hunting season was initiated in
1982. By 1990, a number of newly stocked populations
had become established in eastern Massachusetts.

The first wood stork in recent Massachusetts history
was discovered in Cotuit. Cotuit is a village in the town of
Barnstable, just a twenty-five-minute drive from Woods
Hole. Storks are familiar to most people as very large
white birds that carry human babies in their beaks,
according to fairy tales. The bird in Cotuit is very large,
also very tame, very white with black wing tips, but has no
baby in its beak.

The news of the stork traveled quickly. While not the
first wood stork to appear in Massachusetts, it is far and
away the most cooperative one ever. A wood stork was on

the Vineyard in Chilmark, 26 November 1918. It was shot by a hunter and the specimen was sent to the Boston Museum of Science, #12392. The last time wood storks were seen in the state was 18 November 1963. A flock of eleven birds was seen flying over Plymouth Beach, near where the Pilgrims landed.

There was much bird news on the island this past week but space will only allow a quick sampling. Waterfowl are still the highlight with good numbers of loons and grebes and lots of ducks being seen. While harlequin ducks are more or less routine along the south shore of Chilmark, they are rather rare on the New England coast. The much publicized flock of fourteen marbled godwits of Sengekontacket Pond are still around.

Immature little gulls were seen in Menemsha on the 17th and in Vineyard Haven Harbor on the 18th. These smallest of the gulls are European birds that have recently crossed the Atlantic and now breed on this side of the pond.

29 NOVEMBER 1996

Birds are an integral part of holiday celebrations and the turkey has been the traditional Thanksgiving feast item on the menu since this tradition began. Native Americans who knew all about turkeys long before the Pilgrims arrived, shared their knowledge of these birds and many other things, enabling the first white settlers to survive. History aside, this is a fabulous and invigorating time of year to get outside and move around in the brisk air.

A majestic bird that figures prominently in folklore and fable and today is one of the most sought after by birders has made an appearance in Gay Head. The amazing snowy owl was observed by Albert Fischer in the dunes along the south shore on the 23rd. These powerful birds with large yellow eyes, heavily feathered legs, and penetrating stares are superbly adapted for life on the tundra year-round. Because they live north of the Arctic circle in summer, they experience twenty-four-hour daylight for a couple of months and consequently must hunt in daylight.

Most owls depend on their remarkable eyesight and acute hearing to capture prey in the dark and have evolved special feathering—their own stealth technology—to fly silently and unobserved in the dark. Their only nocturnal enemies are larger owls with the same abilities. Snowy owls have these adaptations plus superior flying skills and large size. They can outfly any other owl and most diurnal raptors.

Snowy owls can capture and eat extremely diverse prey, ranging from mice to Canada geese. They have been observed climbing in direct flight into the sky and killing rough-legged hawks and short-eared owls. They have been caught and banded at Logan Airport in Boston for over ten years, where for some reason they congregate in irruptive years. During this time they have been seen to routinely hunt black ducks, herring gulls, and even to capture and eat great blue herons. Snowy owls have been appearing in small numbers along the coast of New England and more are expected.

Winter

"There is no season
such delight can bring
    As summer, autumn,
winter, and the spring."
        —*William Browne*

THESE ARE THE MONTHS OF HARDSHIP and food short-
ages, cold temperatures and cruel winds. The fight for
survival is on. For animals in the wild, the difference
between life and death can hinge on the minutest of
details, and on luck and circumstance. Some bird species
may trade the hazards of migrating for the perils of staying
put and toughing it out. If it is a mild winter, they will survive. A severe one, the game is over, and Old Man Winter
wins again.

The winter months seem like they should be terrible
for birds and those who watch them, however, many
species are best seen at this time of year. And in the dreary
months bird feeders are the most welcome of diversions.
Lovely energetic birds flit about in an otherwise drab
landscape.

Whether one is watching a feeder or scanning the
waters, winter is an excellent time to learn about birds.
Most are approachable and fairly easy to observe. Waterfowl present a challenge because they are often seen at a
distance, although Farm Pond and Crystal Lake in Oak
Bluffs, Eel Pond and Edgartown Harbor in Edgartown,
and Squibnocket and Menemsha in Chilmark offer close
proximity to many species. Each species has distinctive
shapes, silhouettes, markings, and habits. Once you learn
the basics, buffleheads, scoters, eiders, and mergansers are
quickly and easily identifiable.

Winter is the harshest season. Nature's thinning scythe is honed and great stress is placed on wild plants and animals. Deep freezes and nor'easters take their toll. A strong winter storm will pull in Iceland gulls, who lead an almost exclusively pelagic existence, and lesser black-backed gulls. As the storm abates, even more gulls arrive to avail themselves of food. Anything from benthic organisms churned up and out of where they live, like starfish, sea clams, crabs, and mussels, to small- and medium-sized fish that lingered in too shallow water and were either stunned by temperatures exceeding their particular threshold or caught up in strong currents and battering waves assuages the birds' hunger.

Winter gales also bring about the appearance of alcids. Razorbills—black-and-white football-sized birds—are the most likely. Dovekies and both species of murres occasionally show up.

The incredible buildup of ice that destroyed ancient trees and wreaked unheard-of damage on forests and vegetation over much of northern New England and southeastern Canada in the winter of 1997-1998 was, in human terms, a disaster. In nature's viewpoint, it was a 200-odd-year occurrence. It was part of evolution, much like the "disastrous" wild fires in Yellowstone National Park. These were caused by man's interference with and suppression of the naturally occurring fires that clear away buildups of dead wood before they get out of control, which is exactly what eventually happened. Damage caused by the ice storms was significantly magnified in orchards and monoculture areas of evenly spaced trees and along woodland edges and roads. Just as Yellowstone has flourished with new grasslands and abundant new growth, New England will benefit from its abundant new growth, which will quickly change the landscape. Winter clears the way for the growing seasons.

The abundance of dead trees and broken-off limbs will create new habitats and opportunities for all kinds of life both plant and animal. As a result of the many holes created in forest canopies, more sunlight will reach the ground and many "edge" species of plants and animals will establish themselves. All the early successional plant species will prosper from the increased sunlight and the nutrients returning to the soil. The rapidly growing grasses, annuals, shrubs, and trees will quickly spread, which benefits invertebrates, which in turn feed most of the vertebrate animals.

Suitable nest sites will become more accessible and competition for formerly scarce ones will decrease: a boon to cavity nesting birds (bluebirds, nuthatches, chickadees, woodpeckers, great crested flycatchers, and many owl species) and flying, gray, and red squirrels, porcupines, weasels, and martens.

The abundance of dead and dying wood will provide a bonanza for ground-dwelling invertebrates and nature's recyclers, the amazing array of decomposers. Decomposers are specialized organisms and microbes that exist to decompose or break plant matter down into usable nutrients. By recycling the nutrients, they enrich the soil and benefit the entire ecosystem.

Winter at the higher latitudes of the Northern Hemisphere is a major player in the Darwinian survival of the fittest. Some species, especially birds, have adapted to the changing seasons by being mobile enough to move. Plants revert to periods of dormancy, sometimes dropping leaves, to hunker down and wait it out. The extremes of adaptability are truly remarkable.

December

"The sun that brief December day / Rose cheerless over hills of gray." *—John Whittier*

DECEMBER RIPS BY IN A FLURRY of holiday activities and Christmas Bird Counts. Birding has shifted from automatic attendance at the cliffs at dawn to early morning check-ins with the weather channel. It is not unusual for birders to sleep in. This is the time of year when bird feeder activity greatly increases, particularly when the weather is cold, snowy, or inclement. Sitting in your cozy confines and reading the paper with one eye on the feeder is a reasonable response to the season.

The Vineyard has more birds overwintering than anywhere in New England. Thickets full of seeds and berries sustain many species and also provide impenetrable cover for protection from the weather and hungry predators. The weather is benign compared to the mountains of western Massachusetts, New Hampshire, and Vermont. There is usually less snow cover. The moderating and warming influence of the Atlantic along the south shore makes the Vineyard more survivable for many species.

The waters surrounding the island also provide a bonanza of food for thousands of sea ducks. The Vineyard is just "ducky" for all, but especially the eiders and scoters.

The seas rarely freeze around the island, only an exceptional cold spell (occurring at approximately thirty-year intervals) will punish us to that harsh extreme.

On calm, sunny winter mornings there are lots of birds to be found. Why, even a trek to the dump on Martha's Vineyard can be a fun-filled educational trip—there are always hundreds of obliging gulls to watch. Gulls are varied, fascinating, and have a variety of plumages, which indicate the individual bird's age. They are easy to observe at close range and literally every feather can be seen. All it takes is a bit of interest, patience, and repeated practice to name each one.

The annual Martha's Vineyard Christmas Bird Count is a birding tradition. It is a rare opportunity for a whole army of observers to get out in the field on the same day to areas that often don't merit a second look and turn up some interesting birds.

For an approximate three-week period around Christmas, CBCs are conducted in about one thousand areas in North America and a few dozen places in Latin America. A CBC is a winter census taken within an area fifteen miles in diameter. Ideally, the more varied the habitats included, the greater the number of bird species recorded. Each CBC is held on a single calendar day. Midnight to midnight, twenty-four hours.

Groups of observers attempt to provide uniform coverage of the circle and attempt to count every bird in the circle. Every blue jay, chickadee, loon, etc. At the end of the day all the groups meet and combine their totals. There are approximately twenty-nine CBCs conducted in Massachusetts each year, the results of which are published annually by the National Audubon Society in a special CBC issue.

The Martha's Vineyard CBC is generally held the weekend following Christmas. As the Vineyard is an island, it already has nice boundaries—the shoreline— although it does not fit exactly into a fifteen-mile diameter. But the entire island is covered, and it becomes the only opportunity to document all island bird life on a given day.

How many Canada geese, black ducks, herring gulls, or wintering robins were counted for the entire island? Thanks to the volunteers it is possible to discover trends and get baseline data on winter bird populations for the whole area. Over a period of decades, the results of the CBCs have provided mountains of useful information.

Birders, like birds, have favorite haunts and are creatures of habit. You become familiar with an area and its peculiarities. It gives you a home-field advantage—the more you go out and look, the more exciting sights you will see.

These counts also provide a handy and noble excuse for many people to get out birding for a whole day at a very busy time of year.

---

2 DECEMBER 1994

Occasionally on a trip across Vineyard Sound, a good bird will be spotted from the ferry, but never has this writer

heard of a rare bird being sighted crossing Edgartown
Harbor to Chappaquiddick. Matthew Dix was going to
Chappy on the morning of the 23rd. Looking out the window, he saw a black-and-white bird pop up thirty feet
from the ferry. Even without binoculars, he recognized the
bird as an alcid. It was either a razorbill or a murre. Take a
look in your field guide. The birds are very similar in winter and without a good pair of binoculars or a spotting
scope, caution is the way to go on the identification, especially when attempting to separate the two murres.

Matthew alerted Rob Culbert and Wendy Malpass,
who located the bird at dusk on the 25th with unsatisfac-
tory views. They went back on the morning of the 26th
and were able to find the bird off the Edgartown lighthouse and see the white mark on the gape and the bill
shape that indicated it was a thick-billed murre. The
phones then rattled off the hook. Allan Keith, Gus
Daniels, Arnold and Edie Brown, Tom and Barbara
Rivers, Lily and Eddie Laux and their dad, all want to
thank Rob for alerting them. The bird wanders widely in
the outer harbor and has been seen from the Chappy
ferry all the way out to the red buoy marking the channel
between the Chappy beach club and the lighthouse. It
spends a good deal of time underwater and only pops to
the surface quickly to breathe before it propels itself with
its wings back under water, searching for small fish.

4 DECEMBER 1998
A "huge" little bird was discovered over in Narragansett

in neighboring Rhode Island over the Thanksgiving holiday. The bird is a long-billed murrelet, "big" in terms of its rarity, its range, and recently designated species status. You will not find it in any bird book.

The long-billed murrelet is a small alcid that lives over on the Asian side of the North Pacific Ocean. Little is known about its nesting behavior as only one nest has ever been found. It is believed that it nests either in cavities or on branches of tall trees. Its very similar cousin, the marbled murrelet, nests near the tops of giant redwood trees. Murrelets are common on the ocean where they live and feed, but mysterious in all their other endeavors.

It is believed long-billed murrelets fly into nesting areas after dark and secretly conduct their affairs up in the highest canopy of their respective temperate coniferous forests. Agile and mobile on and under the water, they are clumsy on land and would be an easy target for many mammalian and avian predators in daylight hours. At any rate, this soda can-sized seabird has been wowing birders from all over the country only about thirty nautical miles west of the cliffs at Gay Head.

On and around the island the birding has been very good. Most interesting during the very strong southwest winds recently was the observation of a lone barn swallow flying around the beach at Squibnocket on the 28th. This is a very late record for this species. Slightly more unusual was Allan Keith's observation of a blue-headed vireo at the Gay Head Cliffs on 29 November.

Much more unlikely and unprecedented in the annals

of butterfly records was the observation on 1 December of a giant cloudless sulphur in Lambert's Cove by Simon Hickman. These large neon green-yellow butterflies are tropical and semitropical in origin and rare in New England. Occasionally at odd intervals, they stage irruptive movements north in the late summer and fall.

This year was the largest such movement ever. They were seen right up until the end of October. Yet there were no confirmed sightings for the entire month of November, but several probables. Betsy Cornwall from Chilmark and Edo Potter from Chappaquiddick both saw likely giant cloudless sulphurs separately at different times in Chilmark in November. Both knew they saw something unusual, but were not 100 percent on the identification. Simon, too, knew this was something very different as it flew across his lawn and landed on some flowers that still had blooms.

As an avid reader of "Butterfly Beat" in the summer, he called me and I told him to keep an eye on it and I would be right over. He had carefully placed a crab net over the butterfly as it was sitting on the lawn. I was totally stunned and impressed by a perfect-looking male giant cloudless sulphur. This is a remarkable record for New England. Nice going, Simon!

The first seal and seabird cruises from the Vineyard were conducted this past weekend. The trip Saturday was sunny but windy from the southwest and, instead of fighting the gale force winds, we opted for the waters in the lee of Chappaquiddick, out in Muskeget Channel, and off

East Beach. Great looks at many birds, only a lone grey seal was seen.

Sunday was a peach of a day, and by luck of the draw the participants were treated to calm seas and literally hundreds of harbor seals and about fifty gray seals at close range. No one was seasick either day.

DOVEKIES

The North Atlantic is home to the most amazing little auk, a miniature ecological equivalent to the Southern Hemisphere penguins called a dovekie. The dovekies evolved independently of their penguin cousins by a phenomenon called convergent evolution, and, for various reasons, they kept their ability to fly. On the other side of the Atlantic, they are called little auks, but the latin name is universal, *Alle alle*. Numbering in the millions, they are only eight to ten inches long and nest in a few colonies in the far north.

Dovekies only come to land to nest on scree or talus slopes and cliffs in suitable areas in Greenland and elsewhere in the extreme high Arctic. Then they depart for open water and spend up to nine months in the North Atlantic after breeding. They feed on a variety of plankton, krill, and small fish.

Dovekies are vulnerable on their breeding grounds to predation from native peoples, Arctic foxes, glaucous and great black-backed gulls, ravens, and gyrfalcons to name a few. The birds are harvested by native peoples, including

the Inuit. This has been going on for centuries and has no
noticeable effect on this bird species. Human disturbance in
the form of oil exploration, spillage, pollution, and overfish-
ing is a much more serious threat.

The dovekie is the harbinger of spring and brings great
joy to people in the far north. They welcome its arrival as
we welcome the return of the bluebird. Dovekies come in
clouds, like the driving snow, and fill the air with the uproar-
ious beat of their wings.

In migration or in the winter, which is the only time
dovekies are likely to be encountered in New England, they
are vulnerable to onshore storms, sometimes driven onto
coastal beaches and even far inland. They are able to weather
an ordinary gale, but rarely, such as on 15 November 1871, a
hurricane will force the birds ashore. After this particular
storm dovekies were "wrecked" in every county in Massachusetts and the mortality was high.

Once ashore, dovekies are in serious trouble as they
cannot walk on land or take off unless on water. They become victims of gulls and other predators. Others are
adopted by humans, glad to take a little "penguin" under
their protection. Dovekies are soon killed by this form
of kindness and only have a chance to survive if released immediately in the ocean or other large body of water from
which they can take off.

---

8 DECEMBER 1995

The early morning and evening skies have been exceptionally beautiful this past week. With the still decreasing minutes of daylight, the twilight is much longer and goes through the entire color spectrum. A half hour before sunrise and a half hour after sunset are stunning.

This time of year, there are several species about that are active at dawn and dusk (crepuscular). Much like fish activity at sunrise and sunset, the activity levels increase and normal countershading or camouflage is largely negated by the low light. It makes the prey easier to detect.

Northern shrikes, nicknamed butcherbirds, are robin-sized perching birds with hawklike beaks that nest in the far north and occasionally appear on the island in some winters. They are an irruptive species that invades an area some years, while in other years (most years) there are few or none. This is an invasion year and shrikes are showing up all over New England.

There are at least four different shrikes on the island and possibly many more. They perch on the highest look-out or on telephone wires and feed on small birds and mice. Shrikes are famous for impaling mice on thorns or barbed wire. When mice are plentiful, the birds often leave them in cold storage, for another day. Should anyone find a mouse hanging on a thorn or strand of barbed wire, please call the bird line.

A larger and easier to see crepuscular species is the short-eared owl. These large owls hunt in open fields and along the dunes in search of rodents and anything they can catch. They fly low over fields, resembling giant moths with a distinctive buoyant flight. These owls need to hear their prey scurrying around in the grass and brush, so the less wind the better—dead calm is best.

You can encounter hunting short-ears virtually anytime, although a problem for the owls during daytime hunting is the pesky harassment from crows. On the afternoon of the 4th at 2 PM a lone short-ear was flying around several hundred feet up in the air at Katama being harassed by twenty-five crows. When they do hunt and catch something in the daytime, the crows often steal it. The owls are great flyers, but designed for slow speed and silent flight. The crows can out fly them, especially when in a large group.

19 DECEMBER 1997

For the month that marks the start of the winter on the calendar, December is not bad. With all the bustle of the upcoming holidays and the frenetic shopping and social engagements, the month zips right along. It has also been producing good numbers of birds. This past week was characterized by fabulous weather with temperatures and wind moderate.

A very rare and unusual bird appeared on the stunningly beautiful morning of the 16th in Chilmark. It was sunny, calm, clear, and mild. A lone ash-throated flycatcher was discovered by Lanny McDowell and Richard Greene, off South Road in Chilmark, as it was literally flycatching right around the hardworking duo. Lanny recognized it as a flycatcher in the genus *Myiarchus*, quickly went for his nearby binoculars, and started looking at the obliging individual. It was before 8 AM and the bird was flitting about in the warm sunlight and catching insects. It was picking off very slow-moving flies that were hanging onto the shingles.

There are four species in the genus *Myiarchus* that regularly occur in North America. Only the great crested flycatcher occurs on the Vineyard and it is a common nesting species that quickly heads south after nesting. The next most widespread species is the ash-throated fly-catcher, which breeds as far north as Washington State, but is restricted entirely to the western and southwestern states. The other two are restricted in the United States to southern Arizona and southern Texas.

The ash-throated is differentiated from the similar great-crested by having a whitish throat and breast and much less contrast between the breast and belly. It has a thinner, smaller bill and the birds appear washed out, like faded clothes. The only other island record for this species was a bird on 5 November 1989 at the Gay Head dump by Gus Daniels and Allan Keith.

JANUARY

"In the bleak midwinter / Frosty wind made moan / Earth stood hard as iron / Water like a stone." —*Christina Rossetti*

THE START OF A NEW YEAR is always exciting with visions of sugarplums, i.e. wave after wave of migrant birds flying over the cliffs at Gay Head, dancing in birders' heads. Dreams of extralimital vagrants from distant continents, invading white gyrfalcons from the high Arctic, and porpoising penguins in island waters—it all seems possible at the start of the new year. No dreaming is necessary to enjoy the region's bird life. Reality will set in soon enough, and with it the comforting realization that Martha's Vineyard is a great spot.

Running errands on the island in winter provides a chance to keep binoculars on hand and scout the wires for bluebirds, cedar waxwings, and robins. The winter months show off the impressive numbers of wintering waterfowl and raptors. Loons, grebes, sea ducks, razorbills, and many species of gulls are generally easy to see.

The interface of land and sea, in all its tremendous variety, is a great place to look for birds. It is never better than in the middle of winter, whether along the south shore with roaring surf or the shores of Sengekontacket Pond in

Oak Bluffs. The hard part is keeping fogged-up binoculars and telescopes from obscuring the view, not to mention frozen toes and fingers from obstructing the brain.

With temperatures dropping into single digits and the teens at night, most fresh water is covered with ice. This forces species that prefer fresh water to move to open salt-water. Pied-billed grebes, hooded mergansers, buffle-heads, and the majority of so-called puddle and diving ducks (gadwall, wigeon, scaup, and others) must resort to tidal estuaries or even the open ocean. The longer the fresh water is frozen, the harder it is on these species.

But conversely, the birding only gets better. The birds are concentrated into fewer areas and stay there, since they would never leave a thicket with food, water, and shelter in midwinter. So if a bird is in a particular spot one day, the chances are excellent that it will remain there until mid-March or until something happens to it. "Something" meaning an attack by an avian or mammalian predator, it running out of food, or any number of other disasters. Those of us who feed birds must get up early, especially on the nastiest days, clean the ice and snow off the feeders and fill them. The birds depend on this steady food supply.

Crawl out of bed in the dark and ready your feeding stations, then go back to bed or a favorite window and reap the rewards of your efforts by seeing the throng that arrives. If most of the food in natural habitats is covered, then the feeders become lifelines that will keep the birds afloat (or more accurately, aloft). Eat seeds—live longer. Fresh water is just as important. Birds regulate and efficiently use water, but must obtain it daily. A heated bird bath will be life sustaining.

If the cold continues unabated and the area begins to look like a realm of ice, then new birding opportunities occur. Bald eagles filter down from northerly areas to feed on sick and weakened waterfowl. Bald eagles are undergoing a human-assisted resurgence in New England and are becoming more frequent winter visitors.

Hawks and owls are also big features of the Vineyard in winter, with excellent owling in the state forest and in many wooded areas in the hours before dawn. Hawks can be seen anywhere but the most likely spots are Chappaquiddick, the fields at Katama in Edgartown, the open vistas provided near the Squibnocket area of Chilmark, and Gay Head.

Good news for wildlife is that spring is less than two months away and already the days are getting appreciably longer. Look out over the water in Vineyard Haven Harbor, off the Beach Road in either Oak Bluffs or Edgartown, or anywhere off the south side of the island, and watch sea ducks beginning to display and court. All three species of scoters, eiders, oldsquaws, goldeneyes, buffleheads, and mergansers are already getting paired off. Even in what seems like the dead of winter, preparations for the next breeding season are underway and these hardy ducks will start moving north in just a few short weeks.

1 *January 1996–Hundreds of Birders Flock to Chilmark in Search of Exotic Shorebird.*

The birding community on the island, in the state, throughout all of New England, and indeed the whole country was set ablaze with news of the discovery of a European stray on Martha's Vineyard. A bird species never before seen in Massachusetts was discovered on 26 December 1996 by Allan Keith in Chilmark, which was a rewarding Christmas present for regional birders. The bird is a remarkable large shorebird called the European or northern lapwing (*Vanellus vanellus*). The most migratory member of its genus, it has the longest wings and shortest legs in proportion to its size of any lapwing. The bird has been seen rarely and sporadically in North America. It is one of the most highly sought-after rarities by birders on this continent.

North America is the only continent without a resident member of the lapwing genus. South America has two species and most continents have more. Instead, North America has a gigantic *Charadrius* plover, the killdeer, that has evolved into the vacant lapwing niche.

European lapwings are found primarily on grasslands and farmlands. In Europe the bird descends on farm fields, often in huge flocks. In colder weather they are known to frequent estuaries and tidal flats. The lone bird that appeared in Chilmark has been frequenting, on a schedule known only to itself, the fields at the Keith Farm off Middle Road, in that town. Birders are welcome to watch for the bird from along the vantage overlooking the fields and farm pond from the side of the road.

The bird was discovered at 11:45 AM on the 26th as Mr. Keith was just arriving at his island homestead for a holiday respite. The bird flew by and fortunately was seen by the keenly aware birder, who instantly recognized it for what it was. He ran into the house and telephoned Gus Daniels, who made it to the Keith Farm at warp speed. After getting great views of the bird, they alerted the rest of the island birding community, who decamped immediately for the Chilmark farm.

The phone lines burned all evening and the next day the island was inundated with birders from far and wide. The following morning over a hundred birders were on the first boat and Middle Road resembled something from a science-fiction movie with all the telescopes and camera gear lined up alongside birders on the side of the road.

The fields were constantly scrutinized, but the bird proved elusive. The group was getting mildly despondent when, out of the sky, came the lapwing. The distinctive bird with gleaming white underwings and greenish back had the assembled group oohing and aahing with its every move. The satisfied group dispersed only to be replaced by a larger group of birders that had arrived from as far away as Cape May, New Jersey and New Hampshire.

Everyone who came from off-island to see the bird on the 27th was rewarded with good views. The next day, Saturday the 28th, the bird was not so cooperative. It was seen by several of the top birders in the state at about 9:20 AM, including Richard Forster of Wellesley, Blair Nikula of Harwich, Jeremiah and Peter Trimble of Mashpee, and Jackie Sones of Harwich, who arrived on the first boat. All the other birders that waited all day did not find the bird.

The following day, Sunday the 29th, the bird was not found all morning and most of the day. There were scores of birders waiting. Finally, at 3:15 PM the bird flew in from above, circled the field several times and landed. Those who were patient got great looks at the elusive bird and there were high-fives and backslaps all around.

Massachusetts has a long and rich ornithological history. The oldest bird club in the world, the Nuttall Ornithological Club of Cambridge that meets at Harvard, is here—much to the chagrin of the birders in the United Kingdom. The record of birds seen here is the envy of other states and has been thorough and meticulous. That is why this first documented lapwing is even more significant and exciting.

Historically, there has been a documented invasion of lapwings into North America. In 1927 hundreds were in Labrador and Newfoundland, with some making it into Nova Scotia and New Brunswick. One made it as far as northern Maine on 21 or 22 December 1927 and was seen in a potato field. The only record for Rhode Island is of a bird that appeared on 20 November 1932 on Block Island. There was a lone bird that appeared in South Carolina on 3 December 1940.

Far and away the best place to find lapwings in the United States has been on the east end of Long Island, New

York. Mile after mile of agricultural fields—great habitat for a field- and meadow-loving bird. There have been four records of lapwings in the last hundred years, making it the place for them in this country. From the historical record it seems clear that late fall and early winter are the times for this bird to appear in North America. It is another feather in the Vineyard's cap of great birds. As of this writing on the afternoon of the 31st in a moderate snow storm, the bird has not been relocated.

---

9 JANUARY 1998

Temperatures have been in the forties and fifties and while there has been scarcely any sunshine, the conditions have been remarkably warm and mild for this season. The year has started off more like April than January and the warm, foggy, dismal weather makes it feel springlike. How else to explain the bizarre and unprecedented reports of this opening week of 1998?

Imagine the surprise on Rick Karney's face when he looked out the window at his suet feeder on the morning of the 2nd in West Tisbury and noticed a brown blob a few inches from it on the tree trunk. Was it a mouse or some scat? Grabbing his binoculars, he looked out at a small brown bat resting next to the suet. He got dressed and went out, but the bat had vanished. Could the bat have been visiting the suet feeder? But a bat in January should be hibernating or south for the winter.

Most of the species of bats occurring in this part of the

world are small and brown. The most likely one to be overwintering is the big brown bat, a misnomer, as it is fairly small. Big brown bats are found on the island and do not migrate far from their natal colony. They are to bats what mourning cloaks are to butterflies in New England. Both are very hardy species that stay active late in the fall and start early in the spring. Both are known for being active during warm periods or thaws midwinter.

Brown bats overwinter by becoming dormant. Bats roost in old buildings, attics, belfries, barns, caves, storm sewers, or anywhere suitable protection from the elements and a modicum of warmth may be had. It seems from the evidence that this bat must have been partaking of the suet. Rick has subsequently gone out at night with a flashlight trying to catch the bat in the act of eating, so far with no success. Amazing!

In the same vein of overwintering wildness comes an even more startling report: a whip-poor-will repeatedly calling in Edgartown on 4 January 1998. This is without precedent as these birds are unknown in this part of the world in the winter. It also raises many questions about the species and its ability to practice a form of bird hibernation, going into a torpid state that is known to occur in a western relative, the poor-will. It opens a Pandora's box of questions and speculations that are just the thing to get the new year off to an exciting start.

Sunday, the 4th, was a beautiful, warm, calm, and sunny day. It was ridiculously nice and would have been a great day in April or May, let alone January. Off Race

Point in Provincetown on Cape Cod, Blair Nikula and Jeremiah Trimble found an ancient murrelet diving and sitting on the water not far off the beach. This is a bird of the North Pacific Ocean and only the second one ever encountered in Massachusetts. It was a great find but unfortunately the bird soon disappeared, to the disappointment of birders up and down the East Coast.

That same day Charlie Morano with wife Mebbit, along with Coo Cavallo and wife Donna Goodale, decided to go chase a few golf balls around the golf course. Near dusk, a whip-poor-will began calling. Charlie, not much of a golfer anyway, dropped his club and said, "Holy smokes, that's a whip-poor-will calling" and made everyone listen to this most outrageous bird. It not only has never been recorded before in winter, but it is known to winter from the Gulf Coast south to Central America. What is it doing on the Vineyard in January?

As if those two bizarre occurrences weren't enough, there was other bird news. The Nantucket Christmas Bird Count was conducted on 3 January 1988 and surpassed the Vineyard total by a whopping one species at 127. They had a great count and the two islands are unique in many ways. Nantucket is the best gull-watching locale on the East Coast. On one stretch of beach within a couple of miles were 12,000 Bonaparte's gulls, eight little gulls, three black-headed gulls, seventy-five Iceland gulls, eight lesser black-backed gulls, and many thousands of herring and great black-backed gulls.

There is plenty of bird news for the Vineyard. The

hermit warbler, discovered by Matt Pelikan, is still in evidence at the state forest. A surprise on New Year's Day was a black vulture seen flying all over Edgartown and out near the airport.

Last comes a report of a little black-and-white bird found on the last day of the year at the base of Abel's Hill on State Road. Ruth Kirchmeier was driving along sightseeing with her father when she spotted this tiny bird along the side of the road. Realizing that she needed help, she drove to West Tisbury to get her partner, renowned outdoors writer Nelson Bryant, knowing that he would know what to do. Nelson sagely grabbed a crab net and they proceeded back up to Abel's Hill. Nelson quickly and gently caught the small bird. He recognized it as a dovekie.

Dovekies nest on high sea cliffs and become airborne by "falling" off the cliff until they pick up enough speed to begin flying. They are unable to take off from land. This bird was quickly brought to the land bank property and released on Chilmark Pond. Hopefully it is back out at sea.

26 JANUARY 1996

Looking due west from the cliffs of Gay Head on a clear day you can see the large bridge that spans Narragansett Bay, the Newport Bridge, in Rhode Island. The winds last Friday, 19 January, were fierce from the east and, not far west of the island, catastrophe struck in the form of a tugboat fire and subsequent loss of the vessel's tow. The tow was a barge, longer than a football field, carrying four million gallons of heating oil. The barge floundered in the

face of a stiff southeast wind and came aground very near
shore on a beautiful sandy beach just west of Point Judith,
Rhode Island. It then began to leak thousands of tons
of oil.

As of this writing on the morning of the 24th, the Vineyard is supposedly unaffected, but contamination from
the spill of approximately one million gallons has affected
Block Island and most of Rhode Island's waters. With
strong southwesterly winds predicted for today and later
in the week, the immediate future looks threatening. We
are right in the downwind path of this spill. Oil spills take
a terrible toll on marine life and have long lasting effects
on all aspects of the marine ecosystem.

This may have a devastating impact on Vineyard shell-
fishing and lobstering. Certainly the Vineyard's beautiful
and relatively clean beaches are vital to its economic
health. It would be nice to hear of some kind of plan to
protect these waters, but with nothing done yet, it appears
too late to stop the oil from reaching the island, should
wind and weather carry it here. The response to this kind
of pollution seems to be as good as no response at all. Oil
companies still seem to be getting away with murder, in
terms of environmental damage and their preparedness to
deal with increasing accidents.

Any waterbirds that get oiled are quickly in serious
trouble, since their feathers can no longer insulate them
from the cold water or keep them dry. Most stay in the
water where they obtain all their food and shelter until
they are so drained by the numbing cold that they are

forced to haul out on a beach. By this point most are very weak and sick—prospects for recovery are bleak. Despite rescuers' best efforts, most are doomed.

Visions of the oil tanker *Argo Merchant* grounding southeast of Nantucket in 1976 come to mind. Gus Ben David, director of the Felix Neck Wildlife Sanctuary, was instrumental in dealing with this enormous disaster for all the varied bird life that winters in these food-rich shoals. He developed a method of cleaning the crude oil from the many hundreds of birds with a detergent and other solvents and then putting the birds in a dry, quiet place to recover. He met with some success at saving the oiled birds. This method is being used on the approximately two hundred-fifty birds brought in from the spill in Rhode Island. So far no oiled birds have been found on this island, one can only maintain hope.

Eastern bluebirds and American robins continue to be widely reported on Martha's Vineyard. There is something about bluebirds that is pleasing and unforgettable. Perhaps it is the vivid, shocking, tremendous blue or the beautiful melodious calls. Maybe it is the fact that most people only dream of seeing bluebirds, and when they actually see them, they are taken aback, stunned by the birds incredible presence. The Vineyard is alive with bluebirds these days largely because of the efforts of Paul Jackson, who has a passion for bluebirds. He has single-handedly brought these birds back from the brink of extinction, locally, by placing lots of bluebird boxes in prime sites and preventing house sparrows from taking them over.

Swan Story

The Vineyard had some new visitors that arrived on Sunday,
22 January. While not as exciting for some people as having
the president or royalty, it was, and is, terribly exciting for
those of us afflicted as birders. The visitors were big, white
birds, traveling as a party of three, where no swan of their
kind has ever gone before.

The birds are called whooper swans and they breed from
Iceland, east across the top of Russia to Siberia. They winter
from the British Isles, across Europe and Asia. The only
place they can be found in North America (also in winter) is
on the Aleutian Island chain that runs west from Alaska.
Annually there are ten to twelve birds spread out along this
long, remote, and inhospitable island chain. This is the only
place they occur regularly on this continent and they are not
known to breed anywhere in the vastness of the Alaskan
wilderness, yet.

Whooper swans will not be found in most field guides,
unless you go to the back under the accidentals from Eurasia
section. The only current guide that shows them is the
*National Geographic Field Guide to the Birds of North Amer-
ica.* They are stunningly beautiful birds with an amazing bill
coloration of mostly bright yellow, highlighted with black.

What are three whooper swans doing on the Vineyard in
January and how did they get here? What they are doing

here is easy: feeding like there is no tomorrow. The birds
have been along the south shore of Edgartown in a brackish
pond just to the east of Edgartown Great Pond called Crack-
atuxet. It is a medium-sized pond with good numbers of
mergansers, buffleheads, and mallards, along with at least
one resident and very territorial pair of mute swans.

The whoopers can be seen tipping up and reaching
down with their long necks, feeding constantly. They eat
some kind of grass like kids eat spaghetti. Every so often one
of the mute swans, presumably the male, will come flying up
the pond and attack the three visitors. That's no way to treat
tourists! The whoopers will then scatter, leaving the frustrated mute swan looking confused about which bird to
chase. It will then return to its mate at the other end of the
pond and let the whoopers return to feeding.

The whoopers are nearly as large as the mutes but much
more slender and elegant. When chased by the mute swan or
if alarmed, they call with a remarkably gooselike sound.
When flushed by the mute swan, all three whoopers can be
seen to have no bands on their legs and perfect feathering
with nothing broken or worn.

How these birds got here is easy to answer also: they flew.
Where they came from is the big question. Waterfowl are
kept and bred by various people and institutions around the
world. Anyone attempting to breed whooper swans in North
America would make it known to others and the loss of one
or more birds would be reported. Anyone keeping these large
powerful birds would also clip their flight feathers and band

them. No one keeps fully winged swans.

It turns out that whooper swans have been seen repeatedly in the last three years in Massachusetts. According to Bob Stymeist, active in the *Bird Observer* and Massachusetts bird records, as many as six at a time have been in various New England spots over the past three years.

Three adult whooper swans with no bands were seen in Ipswich, Massachusetts on 31 December 1994. This fits very well with the discovery of the three in Edgartown on 22 January 1995. Wayne Petersen, field biologist and renowned birder, advises that three birds were reported on Long Island in March 1992. They disappeared and within a couple of weeks three birds were photographed in Beverly, MA. The photo indicated some juvenile coloring on at least one bird. The birds moved to Plum Island, disappeared, and came back the following spring. It is high time to look at these birds as not only a records problem but as colonists who have made the jump across the big pond, as they say in England.

Approximately 5,500 whooper swans winter in the British Isles. They breed commonly in Iceland, where they are overprotected. They used to breed in Greenland, but were hunted too heavily by native peoples and are not known to breed there currently. They are large birds, very strong flyers, and could easily make it here on their own. Whoopers could be getting established in North America.

AUTHOR'S NOTE: In 1999, evidence suggests that some whooper swans in the Northeast may have been introduced deliberately by a lone swan breeder.

FEBRUARY

"And in the wood the furious winter blowing."
—*John Crowe Ransom*

FEBRUARY AND THE WINTER DOLDRUMS have arrived simultaneously. Birds are fighting for survival, yet there are signs that winter is coming to a close. The days are getting longer. Dawn and dusk, while always beautiful, are not nearly as dramatic as they were around the winter solstice.

February weather is rapidly changing with lots of wind. The landscape and estuarine zones have "tightened" up, with ice covering many ponds and saltwater tidal areas. One day they will be frozen and ice covered, resembling some primeval scene, and two days later they will be open.

Waterfowl are especially hard hit and are forced to move around searching for suitable areas to feed and rest. Any fat stores they may have had have quickly burned up and every day becomes a life-and-death struggle. Many individuals weaken and a rapid freeze up can trap birds in the ice.

Our national emblem, the bald eagle, welcomes and relishes the hard winter conditions. While impressive to look at, bald eagles are slackers in the hunting department. They would rather have a free meal courtesy of some dead animal than have to hunt and kill a live one. Like beautiful giant vultures, they clean up what is littering the area, and also prey upon wounded or injured creatures. So there is a never-ending feast this time of year to be found in the sick, starving, weak, and injured waterfowl. Many ducks wounded, but not killed, in hunting season eventually become eagle bait.

Frugivores—birds that depend on berries and dried fruits, including robins, cedar waxwings, and yellow-rumped warblers—have a tough time of it. When freezing rain coats their food with a thick layer of hard ice, it renders it temporarily useless, although snow cover makes certain wintering birds stand out dramatically, especially the American robins and eastern bluebirds. There are generally well over a hundred wintering bluebirds and well in excess of a thousand robins spending the winter on the island. Both species have been increasing for the past decade, locally.

Most people still believe in that old wives tale about the first robin of spring. If that were true, then every day on the Vineyard would be the first day of spring as the so-called harbinger is here year-round. The robins that spend the winter here, however, move much farther north to nest in summer, while our breeding robins are spending the winter from the Carolinas to Texas. So while the same birds are not here year-round, the species is always well represented.

Even in the cold, the spring migration gets started with the arrival of the first migrant blackbirds. While small numbers of red-winged blackbirds winter at a few feeders and along the edges of marshes, they still are rare. Normally, flocks of migrant blackbirds arrive during the last week of February, but some years they arrive as early as Valentine's Day.

The advantage to early arrival is that a male bird can beat a potential rival to the best spot. The disadvantage is that weather could freeze and starve them before the season progresses to a friendlier and warmer, more survivable time. There is also less concealing cover and more predators early in the season, so displaying males are relatively easy targets.

A sure sign of approaching spring is the occasional calling of woodcock on warm nights this month. While good weather is infrequent, when and if it occurs these wild and crazy woodland shorebirds will oblige by performing.

―――――

6 FEBRUARY 1998

The first week of February seemed like the first week of April with high temperatures in the forties and conditions that resembled what passes for a Vineyard spring season. However, a look at the calendar indicates it is early February, the shortest and harshest month, and a storm is threatening to envelope the region for several days as this is being written. While bird life is showing signs of spring they must survive the next six weeks. This is not as easy as it sounds.

Food is becoming harder and harder to find for wintering land birds as they deplete the available berries, fruits, nuts, and insect egg cases. A storm with ice and snow cover makes most food items inaccessible and the birds' fat reserves are running on empty. Bad weather now can be disastrous for winterers that are almost over the hump.

Bird feeders become lifesavers for birds displaced because of snow and ice cover. Birds are forced to leave their thickets and travel to find a new source of sustenance, namely feeders. Anyone feeding has a responsibility to provide full feeders and to keep them working properly especially after and during winter storms.

There is great pleasure derived from sitting behind a window, warm and secure, on a cold, windy, stormy, and snowy day and watching the bird feeders. The swirl of action has all the drama one could want. Pick up a pair of binoculars. Look at how fast these birds are living.

The reflexes, skills, and speed with which they maneuver is totally different from our bipedal method of locomotion and earthbound existence. Sit back and watch the show because the roads are probably horrible and there is no sense in going out and playing bumper cars. See if you can determine which birds are male and females. If the birds "freeze" themselves—stop moving, look like bird carvings—surely a hawk or cat is nearby.

The rarest bird in the state, the hermit warbler, continues to remain in a grove of spruce trees in the state forest. Allan Keith and his guests Paul and Francine Buckley had excellent views of the bird on the morning of 1 February.

This group also found a female Barrow's goldeneye and a northern shrike at Squibnocket, and an eastern phoebe, five chipping sparrows, and a couple of field sparrows at the Keith Farm in Chilmark. There are also chipping sparrows in Oak Bluffs.

A snowy owl was seen sporadically on East Beach, Chappaquiddick in Edgartown last week. Paul Schultz saw the bird on the 27th and Matt Pelikan and this writer found it or another during the strong northeast winds on the morning of the 29th. The bird had lots of black feather edges in its plumage indicating its youth. The older they are, the whiter they get. On the morning of the 30th, Susan Yurkus, Janice Callaghan, Nancy Lowe, and this writer could not find the bird again, but we had great views of a perched merlin, Cooper's hawk, northern harrier, red-tailed hawk, and many species of waterfowl.

Great horned owls have been heard calling this past week by Kib Bramhall in West Tisbury and Gus Ben David in Edgartown. They are courting, so this is the best season to hear these powerful birds' booming hoots. Other owl species have a hard time of it at this season.

Marcia Sullivan flushed a large ugly bird off the ground near Scrubby Neck in West Tisbury on the 2nd. It flew up from the ground along the side of the road and landed in a tree. It resembled a turkey. She knew it was something different and thought it was a black vulture, but they are southern birds and not supposed to be around here. She did not know that one has been repeatedly but erratically seen in this area for the past month, flying or sitting anywhere from the Edgartown landfill to around the shores of the Tisbury Great Pond.

Andy Goldman and his son Lee went offshore accompanied by Sandy Lockwood on the 1st. They had a spectacular show of razorbills and black-legged kittiwakes, two pelagic species of birds that are normally seen from land only through the use of a telescope at a distance.

The second-winter Iceland gull that has been near the Oak Bluffs town beach since mid-November is still being seen, especially in an east wind. It is a large individual with a black-tipped yellow bill. On the 3rd Andy Goldman had four tree swallows fly by his house in Chilmark. These hardy birds are feeding on bayberries and if they can hold on another six weeks will be joined by others of their kind returning north for the spring.

9 FEBRUARY 1996

Severe cold, snow cover, and strong winds have put the squeeze on wintering wildlife. Already becoming one of the biggest winters for snowfall since records have been kept, there appears to be no end in sight. For land birds, many food sources that they were using are covered and they are forced to move about looking for anything to eat.

The new snow after the January thaw has again made life hard for hawks and owls that feed primarily on small rodents. Resident barn owls, at the extreme northern edge of their range, are already experiencing a difficult winter with many being found dead of starvation in December and January. Hopefully some of the older, more experi-

enced birds will survive. The older owls have more expertise at where, what, and when to hunt.

Bird migration is at a standstill in mid-February. Aside
from land birds moving short distances to find a new
thicket or feeder, and waterfowl being frozen out of a previously open tidal pond or near-shore location, there is
not much happening. The only notable exception is that
in times of severe cold with increasing ice cover in brackish and saltwater bald eagles appear. These very hardy
birds winter in considerable numbers along the coast of
Maine and, as winter's grip tightens, make it down to the
mouth of the Merrimac River along the shores of Newburyport Harbor and Plum Island just forty-five miles
north of Boston.

Occasionally in severe winters they will travel farther
south along the coast where they are able to feed on waterfowl that are injured by hunters or weak for want of food.
Dead fish along the shore are a favorite food, as are dead or
dying waterfowl. In central Massachusetts, a group of anywhere from a dozen to fifty eagles survive on deer that get
killed and partially consumed by dogs and coyotes on the
ice at Quabbin Reservoir.

American robins and eastern bluebirds continue to be
widely seen and reported. Red cedars, American hollies,
and ornamental crab apples are favorite foods of these
birds, so home owners often plant them, and the birds
flock to them.

With the abundant snow cover land birds frequent the
roads. Birds actually eat sand and gravel to use in their

gizzards to grind up food. They are never more obvious than when in the road. Eastern towhees, white-throated, field, tree, song, and fox sparrows, and several hermit thrushes were all flushed from the road on a recent trip to Gay Head.

The most exciting feeder bird is an immature goshawk that has been seen three times in the past week attacking pigeons in Vineyard Haven. This most powerful of the accipiters is impressive anytime but to see one more than once is just great. Arnold and Edie Brown have this bird frequenting their yard and are not at all upset that it is eating the odd pigeon. It has to eat, too.

12 FEBRUARY 1999

Living and birding on the Vineyard is so good that after a while things begin to be taken for granted. A day in the field with favorable conditions, right in midwinter, reveals thousands of waterfowl of many species and hundreds of loons. Raptors including the spectacular peregrine falcon, merlins, barn owls, and short-eared owls, may be seen hunting.

This winter has been good for alcids. Razorbills have been numerous in the waters surrounding the island particularly after northeast winds.

The seal and seabird cruise went out last Sunday the 7th and participants were treated to exceptionally good weather. Sunny and mild with a light northwest breeze blowing, it was a terrific day to be on the water. Aside from fantastic scenery, good views of many harbor seals and a lone gray seal, and sightings of a merlin, northern harrier, great cormorants, and oldsquaws, the group was treated to a game of "find the miniature submarine" with numerous razorbills.

Razorbills have retained the ability to fly both in the air and underwater. Submerged, they are fast and maneuverable as they zoom around catching small fish. They will often surface in porpoiselike fashion and streak away again underneath the waves in pursuit of fish. When fishing they are underwater 95 percent of the time, so they are often very hard to get a look at.

They have lost much of their agility in the air. On the wing they resemble fast moving flying black-and-white footballs that are sinking. Their heads are higher on the horizontal plane than their aft ends. Their wings seem to fairly buzz at a rapid whirring pace to keep them aloft. They fly, float, and swim south to us in the winter months from breeding areas in Newfoundland and farther north.

Paul Jackson wondered what a lone tree swallow was doing flying in Chilmark around 10 AM on the 5 February. Whether it is an early migrant who had jumped the gun or a previously undetected overwinterer is impossible to say. At any rate probably the same bird was seen by Jamie Cameron, who is visiting the island. Winter's grip is loosening.

The highlight of Jamie's stay to date was a close encounter with a peregrine falcon. On the 8th on the Beach Road in Oak Bluffs he was driving along when he spotted an adult female falcon perched precariously on telephone lines. It was staring down intently. There on the ground was a freshly killed adult ring-billed gull. After watching and waiting about ten minutes, the falcon dropped down right in front of him and proceeded to eat the bird. It plucked feathers, tossing them in the wind, and tore off pieces of breast meat. Nice show!

14 FEBRUARY 1997

The number of people looking at birds on the Vineyard seems to have quadrupled in the past ten years. It is the middle of February with not much going on in the way of entertainment. Nonetheless, everyone has a bird story to tell or questions about an unusual bird at their feeder.

And this month, more than any other, it is a welcome distraction. It gives this writer a chance to talk with people from all walks of life.

Bluebirds continue to be a highlight this winter. The strikingly colored males with the vivid blue and orange-red breasts contrast with the more muted females, which show blue but also gray and brown—a subtler version of the male.

Cooper's hawks continue to be seen and reported. These exciting birds are roughly crow-sized but that is the end of the comparison. These relatively short-winged hawks of the genus *Accipiter* are masters of surprise. They sit perched near the trunk of a tree and when a suitable prey is sighted leap out in direct, fast pursuit. One of their favorite foods is pigeons.

A couple of fortunate observers have seen Cooper's hawks make kills recently. Clem Packish was working in his shop when out of the corner of his eye, he noted some commotion outside. Looking up, he saw a hawk "mantling" a pigeon. The tired hawk had, in a great burst of speed, captured the pigeon and killed it with its talons and beak. The hawk was momentarily resting with its wings spread over the pigeon, when Clem ran out to see what was happening. The Cooper's hawk flew off with the pigeon to eat undisturbed elsewhere.

The dredging along the Beach Road is attracting lots of attention from gulls. Quick to utilize new food sources, the opportunistic birds discovered that where the pipe empties onto the beach there are lots of tasty food items. The gulls are foraging right where the water and dredge material comes shooting out of the pipe snapping up worms, clams, and anything else that looks edible.

They wade in the water just like bears in a salmon stream in Alaska. It seems just a matter of time before rare and uncommon species will appear with the herring, ring-billed, and great black-backed gulls. This spot will be worth checking for the duration of the dredging project.

27 FEBRUARY 1998

The winter of '98 continues with crazy El Niño-inspired weather. Temperatures and conditions, save for an occasional three-day cold spell, have been similar to a typical Vineyard April. The fast-moving frontal system that caused several lethal tornados in Florida moved over and past the island on the morning of the 24th. Peak wind gusts of seventy-two miles an hour were recorded early on this morning along the south shore of Chilmark by Andy Goldman and Susan Heilbron.

The surf and spray were rising thirty feet into the air at the mouth of Oak Bluffs Harbor and conditions there were as bad as this writer has ever seen them. A second-year Iceland gull cruised back and forth effortlessly looking for surf-driven food in the teeth of the gale force winds.

The hermit warbler, the rarest stray bird in the state, continues to be seen in the state forest in Edgartown but is getting harder and harder to find. Many observers have gone in search of this shy and reclusive bird that generally associates with golden-crowned kinglets and come away frustrated. Evidently having exhausted the available food in this area, the bird has expanded its winter foraging area and can simply vanish into the woods.

It was seen on the 16th and 20th by a few lucky observers and Scott Stephens and Penny Uhlendorf finally got a chance to see this megararity. They were afforded great views of this bird with its yellow face, gray back, white undersides, and two prominent white wing bars.

Another rarity that has appeared sporadically but regularly on the island in the past two years was seen again on the 18th. Dick Knight spotted a black vulture hanging around on this drizzly day right near the new agricultural hall in West Tisbury. He phoned Arnold and Edie Brown, who promptly headed straight for this location, and they found the bird sitting on the ground across the street from the Ag Hall on the Panhandle Road.

They called Janice Callaghan, Gus Daniels, and this writer who scrambled to see this elusive and sneaky bird. Gus arrived first and found the bird, keeping watch on it until the others arrived. It flew and perched on the chimney of a nearby home. Thanks to all for such a cooperative effort that resulted in Edie and Janice finally catching up to a black vulture after repeated unsuccessful attempts over the past couple of years.

Gus Daniels had great looks at close range of a drake Barrow's goldeneye off East Chop on the 22nd. He studied the bird in his scope and noted that light conditions were such that the bird's head appeared green, not purple as it normally does. Bright light on glossy colors can look different from every angle. Hummingbirds' gorgets, blackbirds' iridescent heads, and ducks, especially scaup and goldeneyes, can all look peculiar at different times and in differing light conditions.

Red-winged blackbirds have arrived en masse with flocks of males islandwide. Displaying American woodcock have been doing their thing for a couple of weeks on suitable nights. A suitable night is one without a lot of wind or rain, but the determined birds occasionally display even on bad weather evenings and again at dawn.

28 FEBRUARY 1997
The power of the sun is turning back towards the Northern Hemisphere as February turns to March tomorrow.

Earth is spinning and tilting relative to its position to the sun. There is no change of length of day or temperature at the equator but farther away, the higher the latitude, the more dramatic the change. Spring is in the air and the inhabitants of the natural world are well aware of it.

Right on schedule or even a little early this year has been the arrival of red-winged blackbirds. While a small number eke out an existence and overwinter, numbers arrived beginning on the 19th and by the 23rd they were reported in small flocks from feeders all over the island. Mixed in were small numbers of common grackles. American robins are also on the move. They move north very early following the thawing of the ground so that they can get at their favorite summer food, the earthworm.

Cooper's hawks continue to be frequently seen and widely reported. This writer saw four last week in different places: three were adults, one was an immature.

March is here and the return of the osprey, piping plover, oystercatcher, phoebe, and tree swallow is not far off. Meanwhile the waters surrounding the island are full of sea ducks displaying feverishly for prospective mates as their departure date draws near. Loons and grebes are beginning to molt their body plumages and assume their gaudy and spectacular breeding plumages. It is a great time to walk on the beach with binoculars or better still with a spotting scope.

This is a tale of two bird species, well-known and common in the eastern half of North America, who've come together in a unique way. Hybrids between the black-capped chickadee (*Parus atricapillus*) and the tufted titmouse (*Parus bicolor*) have never been reported or documented. The "chickmouse," a previously undescribed hybrid, is readily identifiable as a cross between these two species.

The chance of this occurring between the two species, widespread and abundant over most of their ranges, seems likely but it has not been described before. Taxonomists categorize them not only in the same family, *Paridae*, but in the same genus, *Parus*. (Since this was originally written, taxonomists have put these birds into different genera.) But no one, not even beginning birders, has trouble separating a titmouse from a chickadee.

Black-capped chickadees are widespread in North America, from Alaska to Newfoundland south to central Kansas and central New Jersey, and in the Appalachian Mountains to the Great Smokies. Northern populations are irregularly migratory, but the species is normally unrecorded south of its breeding range in winter. They are abundant on Martha's Vineyard.

The tufted titmouse is a familiar bird also, as it resides in southeastern Minnesota, central New York, southern Vermont, New Hampshire, and Maine south to the Gulf

Coast, and southern Florida. The species is currently in the midst of a northward range expansion. Titmice were considered rare vagrants in Massachusetts until they arrived in the late 1950s. Then they quickly established themselves and colonized the state with the exception of Martha's Vineyard and Nantucket Islands.

Titmice are loathe to fly over water. It is a physical barrier that stops them. They were established in Massachusetts for twenty years before they finally made their move from the mainland of southeastern Massachusetts to peninsular Cape Cod. The Cape is separated from the mainland by a man-made canal that is big enough for tankers and container ships to pass through but generally not considered a barrier to bird species.

Titmice arrived on the Cape in small groups, migrating by day. They did not fly across the canal, but instead funneled over the two large bridges that span the canal. This writer observed them flying over the bridges, above the roadbed, just above the traffic, and under the superstructure. Given this antipathy, tufted titmice are very rare on Martha's Vineyard, a relatively large island with seemingly ideal titmouse habitat. They are common in Woods Hole, Massachusetts, where the Vineyard ferries dock. Although conceivable that a titmouse could hitchhike a ride across on a ferry, it has never been documented.

The shortest crossing from Cape Cod to Martha's Vineyard is from Nobska Point in the town of Falmouth to West Chop in the town of Tisbury, a distance of four miles. This is not far for a bird to fly. A population of common crows commutes daily from Martha's Vineyard to the mainland. The titmouse is a slow flyer and the four miles is a long-distance flight for a woodland-loving nonmigratory species. With no nearby trees for cover or reassurance, it is a frightening ordeal and a huge physical undertaking. Compare it to climbing Mount Everest without oxygen or sherpa guides.

Yet in the past twenty years a handful of intrepid titmice have made the overwater flight. Single birds have shown up at feeders along the heavily wooded north side of the island. They come to feeders with chickadees and then disappear in one to six weeks. Two winters ago a titmouse appeared and visited a feeder a couple of miles from West Tisbury's center.

In February of 1997, I received a call on the bird hot line from a woman with news of a northern gannet. Just before hanging up she happened to mention, offhandedly, that she had had a tufted titmouse coming to her feeder since last November. I'd spent the last twenty years birding intensively on the island and had only seen one. I asked if I might take a peek. She said to come on ahead.

The next afternoon found me standing in the middle of a light snowstorm with extremely cold temperatures up in a remote spot in West Tisbury watching a horde of chickadees and white-breasted nuthatches coming in to feed on sunflower seeds. There were over a hundred individual chickadees in at least four different groups taking turns coming to the feeders.

After about forty-five minutes I caught a glimpse of a

different bird coming in out of the trees with a new group of chickadees. "Here comes the titmouse," I thought to myself. The bird came into the feeder; I got it in my binoculars and was stunned. Here was a bird gray like a titmouse, but with no tuft on its head. It had a black cap, the semblance of a five o'clock shadow where the bib is on a black-capped chickadee, and a faint cheek patch. Wow! The bird flitted off.

I was convinced I'd just seen a hybrid. Only I had never read or heard of such a creature. I needed to see it again. A few minutes later a tufted titmouse, a real one, flew in to the feeder. "Ah-hah, so there really is a normal tufted titmouse." I was reassured, remembering my first Peterson and the description of our only small mouse-colored bird with a tuft on its head.

Shortly, the chickmouse returned and I was able to watch it snatch a sunflower seed, fly to a nearby perch to remove the heart, and then repeat the process three times. The bird was something to behold. A perfect intermediate between the two species. Because of its color and shape, it resembled its titmouse parentage more than the chickadee side of the family. It had a capped appearance and erected a small crest where the tuft should have been.

It was not much of a stretch to conclude it was a hybrid. There are no titmice on the Vineyard, but there are many chickadees. The lone titmouse somehow got itself to the island after crossing open water and was not about to reattempt this feat. After trying for months,

Tufted Titmouse

Black-capped Chickadee

"Chickmouse" MV 1997

"Chickmouse" MV 1998

perhaps years, through more than one breeding season, it was unable to find another titmouse as a mate. Perhaps the following spring the titmouse began seeing promise in the black-capped chickadees and somehow made the leap. The birds are in the same genus.

In titmice and chickadees all breeding behavior is initiated by the males. They are the aggressors who sing to entice a mate and actively court the females. Titmice are larger than chickadees. From behavior studies and available literature, it seems likely that the father of the chickmouse was a male titmouse and the mother a female chickadee.

Something like this is much more likely to occur on an island. Islands are unique. Depending on climate and the distance from neighboring land masses, they can be the most remote outposts on the planet. Separated by water, populations of plants and animals are reproductively isolated from all but their island congeners. Genetic change happens with far greater rapidity in a closed island community than on the mainland. Islands are the key to observing and understanding evolution. Island biogeography and the study of various species, especially island bird populations, was the last piece of the puzzle that enabled Charles Darwin to postulate the theory of evolution. Observing bird life on the remote Galapagos Islands made everything click into place for him.

What happens to the titmouse, chickmouse, and chickadees remains to be seen. Will the titmouse breed

ACKNOWLEDGMENTS

I want to thank the innumerable individuals who have aided and abetted my interest in birds over the last thirty-plus years since this passion began, friends and birders from all over New England and beyond, especially those in Massachusetts and on Martha's Vineyard who have shared their information freely. Unfortunately, I cannot mention all by name since the list would be longer than the book itself, but many are mentioned in the text. These people have allowed me to compile a much more complete picture of birds, even as they have provided interesting tales for my weekly column with its never-ending deadline. Believe it or not, there are some times of the year when bird news is scarce, and without these tips and treasures, my column would be scant indeed.

To Douglas Sands, a now-retired science teacher extraordinaire, who instilled an interest and inspired an eighth grader to look beyond the schoolroom walls and into the natural world. This man is responsible for several generations of birders and naturalists emanating from the Wellesley, Massachusetts junior high school. He could have taught anywhere, at any level, but he knew that he could have the most impact right where he was. He was—still is—right. A couple of his converts include the late Richard A. Forster and Wayne R. Petersen, both former neighbors of mine, who took a teenager under their wings. The birding skills acquired from their combined tutelage and expertise have become a lifelong pleasure.

To Peter Alden, aka Don Pedro, whom I first met as a teenager on Monomoy Island, and has been a friend, travel companion, and invaluable resource. Peter's all-encompassing again with a chickadee this spring? Will the hybrid off-spring be able to reproduce? Will its genes be over-whelmed by the massive tide of chickadee genes? Given that the usual clutch of chickadees is six eggs, with four fledglings—are there other hybrids out there? What do the others look like?

Any discovery brings more questions than answers. Keep your eyes open for this newly described hybrid.

wisdom and organizational skills, combined with his library, make him an unparalleled wealth of knowledge. He is the author of many books, most recently the National Audubon series of regional field guides around North America.

Those fortunate to have traveled with him know he is a tremendous tour leader who thinks first and foremost about his people. If you were traveling to some remote part of the world and disaster struck, as happened to the Antarctic explorer Ernest Shackleton, Peter would get you home. Peter is one of a few who, if kidnapped, blindfolded, and transported to an orbiting spacecraft, then jettisoned back safely to Earth still blindfolded, would not only be able to draw you a map of where he'd landed, he would also know the local birds. Thanks for reading the entire manuscript and making valuable suggestions.

To Blair Nikula, a longtime friend and one of the top birders in the country, in addition to being top "ode" man (as in odonates, as in dragonflies) and all-around naturalist. I am grateful that Blair has made transportation and access to Monomoy and South Beach off Chatham, Massachusetts easier.

To Ken Baum, friend in good times and bad, travel companion, continued source of encouragement, advisor, and wonderful man. Through his efforts and diligence, he has been instrumental in preserving wild places in Kansas and elsewhere. He is a man I admire and attempt to emulate.

To Bill Loughran for so many years of friendship while engaged in birding, bugging, and fishing (mis)adventures. A more fun-loving individual with a zest for outdoor activities would be impossible to find.

To Peter and Jeremiah Trimble for their friendship and sharing their ever-increasing and wide-ranging knowledge and expertise—we have "chased" some remarkable birds with virtually total success. Aside from being two of the finest bird men I have ever encountered, this father-son team knows butterflies, dragonflies, seals, and whales.

To Simon Perkins for decades of friendship and memorable birding on the islands. He is a top-notch field man with total dedication to finding whatever is out there. His historical perspective about birds, particularly in the New England region, is amazing.

To Andy Goldman and Susan Heilbron for their unflagging friendship, encouragement, and help, in particular the magical and frequent pelagic trips aboard their fast and stable boat the *Heritage*. We have seen another world out on the open ocean. Andy has been a frequent traveling companion and harbors a wealth of knowledge about not only birds and fishing, but about living this life.

To George G. "Gus" Daniels and wife Dabby for many years of help and friendship—to Gus for field companionship, expertise, and willingness to help a beginner at writing and editing.

To Arnold and Edie Brown for their friendship, birding companionship, and a variety of things not the least of which was the "loan" of a computer many years ago to help me with my writing. Brownie—here's the evidence that I have been using it.

To Susan Yurkus and her husband Robert, for their friendship and goodwill, countless meals, and for Susan's die-hard field companionship and help.

To Matt Pelikan and his wife Lori, relatively new friends to me and to the Vineyard who have fed, entertained, put up with, and taxied me. Matt is a skilled editor and the winner of a no-reward contest for the subtitle; he came up with "Vagrants and Visitors on a Peculiar Island" as a deadline loomed.

To Jeff Verner and Linda Russell for having always been

generous with their time and for being ready to lend me a hand.

To Michael Wild for being himself. A unique man with the gift of gab, a great friend, and very wonderful human being.

To Wallace and Priscilla Bailey for all the birding opportunities on the Outer Cape, teaching me to drive a standard, overnights on Monomoy, and the memories of working at "Brushfleet Bay."

To James Baird for encouragement, expertise, being a remarkable bird ventriloquist, and all-around fine human being.

To Winthrop "Winty" Harrington for being himself. An astounding individual who is not only a great birder but a dentist that his patients actually look forward to visiting.

To Ted Raymond for being an inspiration to accomplish things and a colleague in the never-ending quest to save natural things. A fine companion in the field or elsewhere, Ted is a man of many talents.

To my favorite lady on Nantucket, Edith Andrews, a giant of an individual in the smallest of physical presences. Edith is a marvel and has forgotten more about birds than I will ever know. She has banded birds "on the Rock" seemingly forever. She imparts knowledge so naturally, you don't even realize you've been instructed.

To another Nantucket favorite, Edie Ray, and her family for their kindnesses, including food and lodging (food, in particular, a much appreciated offering) enthusiastic help, and the sharing of information between our two similar yet very different islands.

To Allan R. Keith for his unbounded energy in the field and dedication to keeping track of what, where, and when. Allan was instrumental in getting me to pay attention to butterflies.

To Susan B. Whiting for all her energy, knowledge of the tour business, as well as her knowledge of Vineyard birds.

To Dick Veit for the times we spent birding on the islands.

Special thanks are due to the staff of the *Martha's Vineyard Gazette* and to Richard and Mary Jo Reston, publishers, and respectively editor and general manager. They have had the good sense to run a column called "Bird News" for decades. They also run other nature-oriented columns, including "All Outdoors" and "Butterfly Beat." The *Gazette* is a newspaper that responds to people's interest in the natural world, and in my eyes, the larger dailies could learn from them.

Nis Kildegaard, news editor, has constantly assembled my writings into some sort of readable form. With an astute knowledge of computers and an eye towards making deadlines more palatable, he has been helpful and encouraging, cheerful and pleasant. He is very good at what he does.

To Laurence Michie for making sense of gibberish on deadline. To Mark Lovewell for his insightful comments. To Glenn Carpenter and Ann Lampson for their cheerful presence at the *Gazette*.

I would like to thank the following for entertaining and useful discussions, experiences in the field and assistance: Denny Abbott, Jonathon Alderfer, Norman Asher, Dave Belcher, Gus Ben David, Catherine Bonham, "Kib" Bramhall, Alice Brown, Janice Callaghan, Jamie Cameron, Ted Camman, Alba Carson, Brian Cassie, Tom Chase, Dave Clapp, Joe Cressy, Rob Culbert, Tom Danforth, Leah Tofte-Dorr, Ken Eber, the late Mait and Helen Edey, Joy Eliasberg, Trevor Lloyd-Evans, Charlie Finnerty, Albert Fischer, Chris and Norma Floyd, Frank Gallo, the late Elizabeth Goodale, Mark Hanson, Brian Harrington, Phillips "Flip" Harrington, Peter Harrison, Karsten Hartel, Marshall Harmon, Steve Hilty, Paul and Mary Jackson, Michelle Gerhard Jasny, Bonnie, Cathy, Marcus, and Marjorie

Laux, Tom Lubin, Wendy Malpass, Whit Manter, Lanny McDowell, Stan Mercier, Mary Mira, Alice Mohrman, John Moore, Charlie Morano, Carl and Sue Mueller, Rich and Ryan McGeough, Seth and Eric Nielsen, Ian C.T. Nisbet, Barry Paulson, Mary Ann Perkins, Barbara Pesch, the late Roger Tory Peterson, Bob and Edo Potter, Richard Pough, Noble Proctor, Marjorie Rines, Tom Rivers, Mark, Cathy and Stephen Robbins, Julius and Judy Rosenwald, the late Dick Sargent, Paul Schultz, Judy Schwenk, the late Manning Sears, Bob Shriber, Ed and Maggie Sibert, Hollis Smith, Jackie Sones, Bruce Sorric, David Stanwood, Bob Stymeist, Rose Styron, Trudy Taylor, Marianne Thomas, Jim Tietge, Peter Trull, Buddy Vanderhoop, Peter Vickery, Eleanor Waldron, Edward O. Wilson, Richard Walton, Ginger Warnes, and Richard Yates.

This book has come to light because of the interest and encouragement of John Oakes, publisher of Four Walls Eight Windows. John read my articles in the paper and was willing to take a chance by publishing my writings in a book.

Last, to my editor JillEllyn Riley for her incredible patience and considerable editorial skills. I had trouble (surprise) meeting the deadlines and she was invaluable in guiding me through the complex maze that is producing a book. She has earned my heartfelt thanks and appreciation.

MARTHA'S VINEYARD BIRDS

This list contains about three hundred regularly occurring species in the traditional taxonomic sequence of families. The list is divided by common family names. This covers the last forty years of the twentieth century. Birds that are currently breeding are annotated with a *BR*.

A list of accidentals (seen fewer than ten times in the last forty years) follows.

LOONS
Red-throated Loon
Common Loon

GREBES
Pied-billed Grebe
Horned Grebe
Red-necked Grebe

SHEARWATERS
Northern Fulmar
Cory's Shearwater
Greater Shearwater
Sooty Shearwater
Manx Shearwater

STORM-PETRELS
Wilson's Storm-Petrel
Leach's Storm-Petrel

BOOBIES
Northern Gannet

CORMORANTS
Great Cormorant
Double-crested Cormorant *BR*

HERONS
American Bittern
Great Blue Heron
Great Egret
Snowy Egret *BR*
Little Blue Heron
Tricolored (Louisiana) Heron
Cattle Egret
Green (Green-backed) Heron *BR*
Black-crowned Night-Heron *BR*
Yellow-crowned Night-Heron

IBISES
Glossy Ibis

WATERFOWL
Tundra (Whistling) Swan
Mute Swan *BR*
Snow Goose
Brant

Canada Goose *BR*
Wood Duck *BR*
Green-winged Teal *BR*
American Black Duck *BR*
Mallard *BR*
Northern Pintail
Blue-winged Teal *BR*
Northern Shoveler
Gadwall *BR*
Eurasian Wigeon
American Wigeon (Baldpate)
Canvasback
Redhead
Ring-necked Duck
Greater Scaup
Lesser Scaup
Common Eider
King Eider
Harlequin Duck
Oldsquaw
Black Scoter
Surf Scoter
White-winged Scoter
Common Goldeneye
Barrow's Goldeneye
Bufflehead
Hooded Merganser
Common Merganser
Red-breasted Merganser
Ruddy Duck

AMERICAN VULTURES
Black Vulture
Turkey Vulture *BR*

HAWKS AND EAGLES
Osprey *BR*
Bald Eagle
Northern Harrier *BR*
Sharp-shinned Hawk
Cooper's Hawk *BR*
Northern Goshawk
Red-shouldered Hawk
Broad-winged Hawk
Red-tailed Hawk *BR*
Rough-legged Hawk

FALCONS
American Kestrel *BR*
Merlin
Peregrine Falcon

PARTRIDGES (GAME-BIRDS)
Ring-necked Pheasant *BR*
Ruffed Grouse *BR*
Northern Bobwhite *BR*
Wild Turkey *BR*

RAILS
Virginia Rail
Sora
Common Moorhen (Gallinule)
American Coot

PLOVERS
Black-bellied Plover
American Golden Plover
Semipalmated Plover
Piping Plover *BR*
Killdeer *BR*

OYSTERCATCHERS
American Oystercatcher *BR*

SANDPIPERS
Greater Yellowlegs
Lesser Yellowlegs
Solitary Sandpiper
Willet *BR*
Spotted Sandpiper *BR*
Upland Sandpiper
Whimbrel
Hudsonian Godwit
Marbled Godwit
Ruddy Turnstone
Red Knot
Sanderling
Semipalmated Sandpiper
Western Sandpiper
Least Sandpiper
White-rumped Sandpiper
Baird's Sandpiper
Pectoral Sandpiper
Purple Sandpiper
Dunlin
Stilt Sandpiper
Buff-breasted Sandpiper
Short-billed Dowitcher
Common Snipe
American Woodcock *BR*
Wilson's Phalarope
Red-necked (Northern) Phalarope
Red Phalarope

JAEGERS (SKUAS)
Pomarine Jaeger
Parasitic Jaeger

GULLS
Laughing Gull
Little Gull
Black-headed Gull
Bonaparte's Gull
Ring-billed Gull
Herring Gull *BR*
Iceland Gull
Lesser Black-backed Gull
Glaucous Gull
Great Black-backed Gull *BR*
Black-legged Kittiwake

TERNS
Caspian Tern
Royal Tern
Sandwich Tern
Roseate Tern *BR*
Common Tern *BR*
Arctic Tern
Forster's Tern
Least Tern *BR*
Black Tern

SKIMMERS
Black Skimmer *BR*

ALCIDS (PUFFINS)
Dovekie
Common Murre
Thick-billed Murre
Razorbill

PIGEONS AND DOVES
Rock Dove *BR*
Mourning Dove *BR*

CUCKOOS
Black-billed Cuckoo *BR*
Yellow-billed Cuckoo *BR*

BARN OWLS
Barn Owl *BR*

OWLS
Eastern Screech-Owl *BR*
Great Horned Owl *BR*
Snowy Owl
Long-eared Owl *BR*
Short-eared Owl *BR*
Northern Saw-whet Owl *BR*

**NIGHTJARS
(CAPRIMULGIDS)**
Common Nighthawk
Chuck-will's-widow *BR*
Whip-poor-will *BR*

SWIFTS
Chimney Swift *BR*

HUMMINGBIRDS
Ruby-throated Hummingbird *BR*

KINGFISHERS
Belted Kingfisher *BR*

WOODPECKERS
Red-headed Woodpecker

Red-bellied Woodpecker *BR*
Yellow-bellied Sapsucker
Downy Woodpecker *BR*
Hairy Woodpecker *BR*
Northern (Yellow-shafted)
  Flicker *BR*

TYRANT-FLYCATCHERS
Olive-sided Flycatcher
Eastern Wood-Pewee *BR*
Yellow-bellied Flycatcher
Acadian Flycatcher *BR*
Alder Flycatcher
Willow Flycatcher *BR*
Least Flycatcher
Eastern Phoebe *BR*
Great Crested Flycatcher *BR*
Western Kingbird
Eastern Kingbird *BR*

LARKS
Horned Lark *BR*

SWALLOWS
Purple Martin
Tree Swallow *BR*
Northern Rough-winged
Swallow *BR*
Bank Swallow *BR*
Cliff Swallow
Barn Swallow *BR*

CROWS AND JAYS
Blue Jay *BR*
American Crow *BR*

CHICKADEES (TITMICE)
Black-capped Chickadee *BR*

NUTHATCHES
Red-breasted Nuthatch *BR*
White-breasted Nuthatch *BR*

CREEPERS
Brown Creeper *BR*

WRENS
Carolina Wren *BR*
House Wren *BR*
Winter Wren
Marsh Wren

KINGLETS
Golden-crowned Kinglet *BR*
Ruby-crowned Kinglet

OLD WORLD WARBLERS
Blue-gray Gnatcatcher *BR*

THRUSHES
Eastern Bluebird *BR*
Veery *BR*
Gray-cheeked/Bicknell's Thrush
Swainson's Thrush
Hermit Thrush *BR*
Wood Thrush *BR*
American Robin *BR*

MOCKINGBIRDS (MIMIC THRUSHES)
Gray Catbird *BR*
Northern Mockingbird *BR*
Brown Thrasher *BR*

PIPITS
American Pipit

WAXWINGS
Cedar Waxwing *BR*

SHRIKES
Northern Shrike

STARLINGS
European Starling (Sky-rat) *BR*

VIREOS
White-eyed Vireo *BR*
Blue-headed (Solitary) Vireo
Yellow-throated Vireo
Warbling Vireo *BR*
Philadelphia Vireo
Red-eyed Vireo *BR*

AMERICAN WARBLERS (WOOD WARBLERS)
Blue-winged Warbler *BR*
Golden-winged Warbler
Tennessee Warbler
Orange-crowned Warbler
Nashville Warbler

Northern Parula *BR*
Yellow Warbler *BR*
Chestnut-sided Warbler *BR*
Magnolia Warbler
Cape May Warbler
Black-throated Blue Warbler
Yellow-rumped (Myrtle) Warbler
Black-throated Green
  Warbler *BR*
Blackburnian Warbler
Yellow-throated Warbler
Prairie Warble *BR*
Palm Warbler
Bay-breasted Warbler
Blackpoll Warbler
Cerulean Warbler
Black-and-white Warbler *BR*
American Redstart *BR*
Prothonotary Warbler
Worm-eating Warbler
Ovenbird *BR*
Northern Waterthrush
Louisiana Waterthrush
Kentucky Warbler
Connecticut Warbler
Mourning Warbler
Common Yellowthroat *BR*
Hooded Warbler
Wilson's Warbler
Canada Warbler
Yellow-Breasted Chat

TANAGERS
Summer Tanager
Scarlet Tanager *BR*

CARDINALS (FINCHES
AND GROSBEAKS)
Northern Cardinal *BR*
Rose-breasted Grosbeak
Blue Grosbeak
Indigo Bunting
Dickcissel

AMERICAN SPARROWS
(FINCHES)
Eastern (Rufous-sided)
  Towhee *BR*
American Tree Sparrow
Chipping Sparrow *BR*
Clay-colored Sparrow
Field Sparrow *BR*
Vesper Sparrow
Lark Saprrow
Savannah Sparrow *BR*
Grasshopper Sparrow *BR*
Salt Marsh Sharp-tailed
  Sparrow *BR*
Fox Sparrow
Song Sparrow *BR*
Lincoln's Sparrow
Swamp Sparrow
White-throated Sparrow
White-crowned Sparrow
Dark-eyed (Slate-colored) Junco
Lapland Longspur
Snow Bunting

BLACKBIRDS (ICTERIDS)
Bobolink
Red-winged Blackbird *BR*
Eastern Meadowlark *BR*
Yellow-headed Blackbird
Rusty Blackbird
Common (Eastern) Grackle *BR*
Brown-headed Cowbird *BR*
Orchard Oriole *BR*
Baltimore (Northern) Oriole *BR*

FINCHES
Purple Finch *BR*
House Finch *BR*
Red Crossbill
White-winged Crossbill

Common Redpoll
Pine Siskin
American Goldfinch *BR*
Evening Grosbeak

OLD WORLD SPARROWS
House (English) Sparrow aka
 Limey *BR*

ACCIDENTALS
(number of records in forty years, and year last recorded follows)

Pacific (Arctic) Loon	6	1997
Eared Grebe	1	1991
Western Grebe	2	1969
Albatross, species	2	1995
Audubon's Shearwater	2	1967
Red-billed Tropicbird	2	1988
American White Pelican	3	1994
Brown Pelican	3	1988
Least Bittern	4	1985
Reddish Egret	1	1992
Fulvous Whistling-Duck	2	1974

Cinnamon Teal	1	1983
Swallow-tailed Kite	4	1996
Mississippi Kite	1	1989
Swainson's Hawk	2	1975
Golden Eagle	3	1994
Yellow Rail	2	1973
Clapper Rail	4	1998
Purple Gallinule	6	1985
Sandhill Crane	2	1984
Northern Lapwing	1	1996
Wilson's Plover	5	1985
Black-necked Stilt	3	1982
American Avocet	3	1970
Eurasian Curlew	1	1978
Long-billed Curlew	2	1990
Bar-tailed Godwit	1	1968
Sharp-tailed Sandpiper	1	1992
Curlew Sandpiper	2	1967
Ruff	6	1986
Long-billed Dowitcher	6	1997
Long-tailed Jaeger	5	1991
Franklin's Gull	2	1992
Sabine's Gull	3	1988
Gull-billed Tern	6	1996
Bridled Tern	3	1991
Sooty Tern	7	1991
Black Guillemot	4	1992
Atlantic Puffin	5	1995
White-winged Dove	2	1988
European (Common) Cuckoo	1	1981
Northern Hawk Owl	1	1966
Burrowing Owl	2	1986
European (Common/The) Swift	1	1996

Black-backed Woodpecker	5	1965
Say's Phoebe	2	1978
Ash-throated Flycatcher	3	1998
Sulphur-bellied Flycatcher	1	1984
Gray Kingbird	1	1988
Scissor-tailed Flycatcher	8	1998
Fork-tailed Flycatcher	2	1961
Tufted Titmouse	8	1997
Sedge Wren	2	1992
Townsend's Solitaire	1	1982
Varied Thrush	3	1992
Bohemian Waxwing	2	1966
Loggerhead Shrike	9	1988
Black-throated Gray Warbler	2	1996
Townsend's Warbler	1	1998
Hermit Warbler	1	1998
Western Tanager	5	1992
Black-headed Grosbeak	3	1988
Painted Bunting	2	1982
Lark Bunting	2	1989
Henslow's Sparrow	5	1997
LeConte's Sparrow	1	1998
Harris' Sparrow	5	1984
Western Meadowlark	1	1967
Brewer's Blackbird	7	1997
Pine Grosbeak	9	1966